MUSLIM AMERICANS IN THE MILITARY

MUSLIM AMERICANS IN THE MILITARY

CENTURIES OF SERVICE

EDWARD E. CURTIS IV

INDIANA UNIVERSITY PRESS
Bloomington and Indianapolis

This book is a publication of

Indiana University Press
Office of Scholarly Publishing
Herman B Wells Library 350
1320 East 10th Street
Bloomington, Indiana 47405 USA

iupress.indiana.edu

The paper used in this publication meets the minimum requirements of
the American National Standard for Information Sciences—Permanence
of Paper for Printed Library Materials, ANSI Z39.48-1992.

Manufactured in the United States of America

Names: Curtis, Edward E., author.
Title: Muslim Americans in the military : centuries of service /
    Edward E. Curtis IV.
Description: Bloomington : Indiana University Press, 2016. |
    Includes index.
Identifiers: LCCN 2016041283 | ISBN 9780253027177 (pbk. : alk. paper)
Subjects: LCSH: Muslim soldiers—United States—History. |
    Muslims—United States—History. | United States—Armed
    Forces—Religious life. | Soldiers—Religious life—United States.
Classification: LCC E184.M88 C876 2016 |
    DDC 355.0088/2970973—dc23
LC record available at https://lccn.loc.gov/2016041283

1 2 3 4 5   21 20 19 18 17 16

To all families living with Rett Syn

CONTENTS

ACKNOWLEDGMENTS

THIS BOOK WAS THE IDEA of Ashley Runyon and her team at Indiana University Press, and I am thankful that they asked me to write it. David Hulsey, Michelle Sybert, Anna Francis, and Dee Mortensen were encouraging and helpful throughout the process. Peggy Solic offered essential assistance with illustrations and other aspects of the project. Rachel Rosolina was an effective project manager and a wonderful copyeditor.

I am deeply grateful to Imam Michael Saahir of Nur Allah Islamic Center in Indianapolis. He connected me with S.Sgt. Lyndon Bilal, commander of the Muslim American Veterans Association, and Bilal then put me in touch with Col. Nashid Salahuddin, Lt. Col. Shareda Hosein, and Lt. Col. Abdul-Rasheed Muhammad. Bilal also shared some important photographs from his own archive.

Mansoor Shams kindly put me in touch with Harris Khan.

My colleagues, Prof. Harvey Stark and Dr. Jeffrey Diamant, shared their research on Muslims in the military.

My colleague, Andrea Jain, helped me think though some of this material, and David Craig gave me lots of encouragement.

Filmmaker David Washburn, who is making a documentary on the subject, gave me advice, suggested contacts, and was generous with materials. In Indianapolis, Muslim Alliance of Indiana director Rima Khan Shahid, Muzaffar Ahmad, Muhammad Safder, and Shariq Siddiqui were willing to help.

My colleague, Jane Schultz, author of *Women at the Front: Hospital Workers in Civil War America* and historical adviser to the PBS series *Mercy Street*, translated the Civil War–era cursive on one of Nicholas Said's military records and then explained to me what it probably meant. Precious Rasheeda Muhammad, the "Muslim History Detective," was willing to field inquiries about Said.

Doug Baum of the Texas Camel Corps talked to me about Hadji Ali. Philip Goff looked for some mention of Muslim troops in some Revolutionary War–era diaries. A long time ago, librarians at the State Historical Society of North Dakota photocopied interviews with Syrian and Lebanese settlers from their Ethnic History Files; I did not realize at the time that they would help me write the history of Muslim service members in World War I.

My family put up with me working some on the weekends to get this done quickly, and I am so grateful that it was only for a little while.

A portion of my royalties for this book will go to Rettsyndrome.org, which funds research and assists families living with Rett Syndrome. Rett Syndrome is a devastating neurological disorder that mainly affects young girls. In the case of our family, and many others, our daughter lost her ability to talk, walk, and use her hands in any effective way. But she understands everything going on around her, is incredibly social, and loves to go to school and play with her friends. Since the gene associated with Rett Syndrome has been identified—it was discovered by neuroscientist Dr. Huda Zoghbi—we have hope that one day a cure will be found.

MUSLIM AMERICANS IN THE MILITARY

CENTURIES OF SERVICE

EDWARD E. CURTIS IV

INDIANA UNIVERSITY PRESS

Bloomington and Indianapolis

This book is a publication of

Indiana University Press
Office of Scholarly Publishing
Herman B Wells Library 350
1320 East 10th Street
Bloomington, Indiana 47405 USA

iupress.indiana.edu

The paper used in this publication meets the minimum requirements of
the American National Standard for Information Sciences—Permanence
of Paper for Printed Library Materials, ANSI Z39.48-1992.

Manufactured in the United States of America

Names: Curtis, Edward E., author.
Title: Muslim Americans in the military : centuries of service /
    Edward E. Curtis IV.
Description: Bloomington : Indiana University Press, 2016. |
    Includes index.
Identifiers: LCCN 2016041283 | ISBN 9780253027177 (pbk. : alk. paper)
Subjects: LCSH: Muslim soldiers—United States—History. |
    Muslims—United States—History. | United States—Armed
    Forces—Religious life. | Soldiers—Religious life—United States.
Classification: LCC E184.M88 C876 2016 |
    DDC 355.0088/2970973—dc23
LC record available at https://lccn.loc.gov/2016041283

1 2 3 4 5   21 20 19 18 17 16

To all families living with Rett Syndrome

CONTENTS

ACKNOWLEDGMENTS

THIS BOOK WAS THE IDEA of Ashley Runyon and her team at Indiana University Press, and I am thankful that they asked me to write it. David Hulsey, Michelle Sybert, Anna Francis, and Dee Mortensen were encouraging and helpful throughout the process. Peggy Solic offered essential assistance with illustrations and other aspects of the project. Rachel Rosolina was an effective project manager and a wonderful copyeditor.

I am deeply grateful to Imam Michael Saahir of Nur Allah Islamic Center in Indianapolis. He connected me with S.Sgt. Lyndon Bilal, commander of the Muslim American Veterans Association, and Bilal then put me in touch with Col. Nashid Salahuddin, Lt. Col. Shareda Hosein, and Lt. Col. Abdul-Rasheed Muhammad. Bilal also shared some important photographs from his own archive.

Mansoor Shams kindly put me in touch with Harris Khan.

My colleagues, Prof. Harvey Stark and Dr. Jeffrey Diamant, shared their research on Muslims in the military.

My colleague, Andrea Jain, helped me think though some of this material, and David Craig gave me lots of encouragement.

Filmmaker David Washburn, who is making a documentary on the subject, gave me advice, suggested contacts, and was generous with materials. In Indianapolis, Muslim Alliance of Indiana director Rima Khan Shahid, Muzaffar Ahmad, Muhammad Safder, and Shariq Siddiqui were willing to help.

My colleague, Jane Schultz, author of *Women at the Front: Hospital Workers in Civil War America* and historical adviser to the PBS series *Mercy Street*, translated the Civil War–era cursive on one of Nicholas Said's military records and then explained to me what it probably meant. Precious Rasheeda Muhammad, the "Muslim History Detective," was willing to field inquiries about Said.

Doug Baum of the Texas Camel Corps talked to me about Hadji Ali. Philip Goff looked for some mention of Muslim troops in some Revolutionary War–era diaries. A long time ago, librarians at the State Historical Society of North Dakota photocopied interviews with Syrian and Lebanese settlers from their Ethnic History Files; I did not realize at the time that they would help me write the history of Muslim service members in World War I.

My family put up with me working some on the weekends to get this done quickly, and I am so grateful that it was only for a little while.

A portion of my royalties for this book will go to Rettsyndrome.org, which funds research and assists families living with Rett Syndrome. Rett Syndrome is a devastating neurological disorder that mainly affects young girls. In the case of our family, and many others, our daughter lost her ability to talk, walk, and use her hands in any effective way. But she understands everything going on around her, is incredibly social, and loves to go to school and play with her friends. Since the gene associated with Rett Syndrome has been identified—it was discovered by neuroscientist Dr. Huda Zoghbi—we have hope that one day a cure will be found.

MUSLIM AMERICANS IN THE MILITARY

ONE

TWO FALLEN SOLDIERS NAMED KHAN

ARMY RESERVES CAPTAIN HUMAYUN KHAN, twenty-seven years old, knew that sacrifice might be required.

Could he know how symbolic that sacrifice would become?

It was his day off, but Khan wanted to check on the troops under his command. His mission, according to Khan's senior officer, retired Maj. Gen. Dana J. H. Pitard, was to protect wheeled convoys and guard the gates of Forward Operating Base Warhorse in eastern Iraq. "The 201st Forward Support Battalion, Humayun's unit," later wrote Pitard, "was the most motivated and combat-oriented logistics unit I had ever seen."

More than one thousand Iraqis worked at Camp Warhorse, and Khan's unit was responsible for inspecting their cars. According to Pitard, "We had killed or wounded several innocent Iraqi drivers at our gates over the previous month for failing to heed our warning signs and our gate guards' instructions." But Khan consistently worked to improve relations with the Iraqi workers and would do everything possible to prevent further accidents.

Khan worked from midnight to noon on June 7, 2004, and he was tired. Sgt. Crystal Shelby spoke freely with him, telling him that he needed to get some rest before working further.

But Khan insisted, as he was worried. Shelby drove him to the base entrance.

Khan was well-liked among his troops in the 201st Forward Support Battalion, First Infantry. According to S.Sgt. Marie Legros, he was a "soldier's soldier . . . just that type of person, wanting to make sure his soldiers were okay."

Sgt. Laci Walker said that he "never put his rank about his care for his soldiers and comrades." Khan would throw an extra towel to someone in need, and he made sure that everyone knew they could steal sandwich condiments from his personal stash.

He tried to protect troops in harm's way, putting himself between those under his command and the danger.

Soon after arriving at the base entrance on June 8, 2004, he saw an orange taxi winding its way through the gate's serpentine barriers. This was during "the morning rush" at Camp Warhorse, when Iraqi workers would enter the base. Khan ordered his solders to get down. He walked toward the vehicle and gestured to the driver, indicating that he should stop. "Humayun probably moved toward the suspicious vehicle to avoid killing the driver unnecessarily," reasoned Pitard.

A bomb detonated.

It killed Khan, two Iraqi civilians, and two insurgents.[1]

Khan was laid to rest in Arlington National Cemetery with full military honors and Islamic funeral prayers. He was awarded a Bronze Star, a military medal for heroism, and a Purple Heart, the medal given to armed service members who were killed or injured in the line of duty.

Capt. Humayun Saqib Muazzam Khan (1976–2004) was one of three to six million Americans who identify as Muslim, followers of the religion of Islam. Born in the United Arab Emirates, where his family was living at the time, he traced his roots to Pakistan, a country inhabited by about 10 percent of all the world's Muslims, around 167 million people. About one quarter of all Muslims in the United States have ethnic roots in South Asia, which includes the countries of Pakistan, Bangladesh, India, and depending on who is counting, Afghanistan.[2]

South Asian American Muslims are among the approximately four thousand active duty military members—and a perhaps a couple thousand more in the reserves—who identify themselves officially on Department of Defense documents as Muslims.

Khan was also one of over a dozen Muslims who gave his life in the post–9/11 era as a member of the armed forces.

He came to the United States as a little boy and grew up around the Greater Washington, DC, area. Khan graduated from John F. Kennedy High School in Silver Spring, Maryland, in 1996, and went to college at the University of Virginia. He enrolled in the US Army's Reserve Officers' Training Corps (ROTC), which trains future officers while they are still in college. He wanted to become a lawyer.[3]

Khizr and Ghazala Khan, parents of the late Capt. Humayun Khan, appeared at the last night of the 2016 Democratic National Convention to endorse Democratic candidate Hillary Clinton. (REUTERS / Lucy Nicholson / Alamy Stock Photo.)

Khan graduated from the University of Virginia in 2000 and was planning on attending law school.

And then came the terrorist attacks of September 11, 2001, and subsequent wars in Afghanistan (2001) and Iraq (2003).[4]

Khan had to delay his plans for law school. In 2002, he was posted to Vilseck, Germany, and during a visit to a local Bavarian café, he struck up a conversation with a German woman named Irene Auer. "He had a beautiful voice," she remembered.

Khan and Auer began dating, spending weekends together in his apartment, which was located outside the base. They enjoyed debating everything from the meaning of life to the war in Iraq. Auer was opposed to the US invasion; Khan said that he would do his duty. "You know that I am married," he said jokingly to Auer. "I am married to the US Army."

When his mother, Ghazala Khan, visited him in 2003, he introduced his girlfriend to her. Then, Auer flew to the United States to meet his father, Khizr Khan. By the time Khan had to leave for Iraq on February 9, 2004, they had decided to get married. An email from Iraq encouraged Auer to pick out her engagement ring.[5]

Shortly after, Khan was killed.

A dozen years later, this soldier's sacrifice was transformed into a political symbol during the US presidential contest between Democrat Hillary Clinton and Republican Donald Trump. Capt. Humayun Khan's story became a debate over what it means to be an American.

On the final night of the 2016 Democratic National Convention, Khizr Khan gave a speech immediately before Chelsea Clinton, who introduced her mother, Hillary Clinton. The fact that the speech was given so close to the candidate's acceptance speech itself shows just how important the message was to the candidate's campaign.

Ghazala Khan stood next to her husband. She was wearing a blue, loose-fitting headscarf that partially covered her hair—a typical Pakistani style also worn by former Prime Minister of Pakistan, Benazir Bhutto. Khizr Khan wore a dark suit and blue necktie. (Blue is the color of the Democratic Party.)

He began his speech by acknowledging the service of all veterans and all those still in military uniform, saying that he and his wife were "patriotic American Muslims with undivided loyalty to our country." His meaning was clear: some Americans may think you cannot be Muslim and American, and he wanted to correct that.

He went on to identify himself with other important American symbols—immigrant success, democracy, and hard work. Then came praise of Hillary Clinton and criticism of Donald Trump. In an earlier speech, Clinton had called Capt. Khan "the best of America."

But if it were up to Donald Trump, Khizr Khan said, his son would never have been permitted to immigrate to the United States, referring to Trump's proposal to ban Muslims from entering the country.

In one of the most dramatic gestures of the 2016 Democratic National Convention, Khizr Khan reached into his pocket to grab a small copy of the US Constitution. He was known to carry them around with him at all times, offering a copy to people who visited him.

"Let me ask you," he challenged Trump, "have you ever read the US Constitution? I will gladly lend you my copy."

He continued his attack on Trump, saying, "Have you ever been to Arlington Cemetery?" He described the diversity of people who had sacrificed their lives for the United States. "You have sacrificed nothing and no one," he said.[6]

Interviewed by George Stephanopoulos of ABC News two days afterward, Trump responded to a question about Khizr Khan's speech by referring to Ghazala Khan. "If you look at his wife," Trump commented, "she was standing there. She had nothing to say. She probably—maybe she wasn't allowed to say. You tell me. But plenty of people have written that. She was extremely quiet. And it looked like she had nothing to say."

In Trump's formulation, the mother of a fallen soldier, standing next to her husband, became another kind of symbol. A symbol of the oppressed, silent Muslim woman. That stereotype continues to resound in US politics and is often an effective appeal—used by both conservatives and liberals—on behalf of US foreign policy in Muslim-majority countries. The Muslim woman in need of saving has been offered more than once as a reason to go to war.

In this case, however, it not only offended Muslims and those sympathetic to their plight, but it also awoke conservative voices who saw Ghazala Khan not so much as an oppressed Muslim woman but instead as the mother of a soldier killed while serving his country.

"My family has been Republican ever since my maternal grandparents migrated from Jim Crow South Carolina to Philadelphia in the late 1920s," wrote Maj. Gen. Pitard. But for Pitard, a lack of respect for Khan's family was a matter that transcended political party: "I join all those who stand in support of the Khan family. This family is our family, and any attack on this wonderful American Gold Star family is an attack on all patriotic and loyal Americans who have sacrificed to make our country great."

Without ever mentioning Donald Trump by name, the general made clear Trump had gone too far. He even turned Trump's campaign slogan, "Make America Great Again," against Trump, echoing the claim from Khizr Khan's speech that Trump had not worn the uniform in defending the United States. Just in case his meaning was unclear, Pitard concluded, "Any politically or racially motivated attack on the Khans is despicable and un-American."[7]

Ghazala Khan had her own response to Trump. "Donald Trump said I had nothing to say," she wrote in a *Washington Post* op-ed. "I do." She lovingly eulogized her son and explained why she did not speak at the Democratic National Convention:

Every day I feel the pain of his loss. It has been 12 years, but you know hearts of pain can never heal as long as we live. Just talking about it is hard for me all the time. Every day, whenever I pray, I have to pray for him, and I cry. The place that emptied will always be empty. I cannot walk into a room with pictures of Humayun. For all these years, I haven't been able to clean the closet where his things are—I had to ask my daughter-in-law to do it. Walking onto the convention stage, with a huge picture of my son behind me, I could hardly control myself. What mother could? Donald Trump has children whom he loves. Does he really need to wonder why I did not speak?[8]

She said that she had been offered the podium but declined to speak. She was utterly unable to do so because of her grief.

Trump stopped talking about the incident. What more could he say? But in the aftermath of Trump's criticism, social and traditional media were abuzz as ordinary citizens and politicians alike sought to weigh in, duck out, and manage what became a public relations problem for the Republican nominee. While many of Trump's supporters came to his aid and kept up both personal and political attacks on the Khan family and Clinton's pro-Muslim stance, they seemed to be in the minority. The decision by Clinton's campaign to feature the Khans prominently at the convention was a smart move. It had enormous political payoff because it helped make Clinton's case that her opponent's ideas were un-American.

On this issue, at least, Clinton had found the political center. She did so by uplifting the fallen Muslim American soldier as a symbol of a "good Muslim" who can also be American. In addition, Clinton regularly denounced anti-Muslim prejudice in her campaign. Once again, the issue was what it meant to be an American. Clinton did so out of her commitment to religious freedom, a most American idea.

The difference between Clinton and her Republican rival was that she was willing to include Muslim Americans in her vision of US national identity. She echoed what historians call the "liberal consensus" during the Cold War that was supported by Republican President and former Supreme Allied Commander Gen. Dwight D. Eisenhower. This consensus offered Jews, Muslims, and other religious minorities a pact: if you believe in God—however you conceive of God—and are willing to defend the flag against communism and other security threats, then you, too, are American and are entitled to the accompanying rights and privileges.

It is not an accident that Eisenhower was the first US president to laud the opening of a mosque in the United States. His 1957 visit to the Islamic Center on Massachusetts Avenue in Washington, DC, was a powerful symbol of the bargain that the United States was willing to make with religious minorities—but not yet racial or sexual minorities. "I should like to assure you, my Islamic [Muslim] friends, that under the American Constitution, under American tradition, and in American hearts," Eisenhower said, "this Center, this place of worship is just as welcome as could be a

similar edifice of any other religion." Eisenhower made clear in other set-
tings that he wanted Muslim allies in the Cold War with the Soviet Union.
That meant including them in the notion of American national identity.
"Indeed," he continued, "America would fight with her whole strength
for your right to have here your own church [religious congregation] and
worship according to your own conscience. This concept is indeed part
of America, and without that concept we would be something else than
what we are."[9]

But with the onset of the post–9/11 wars on terrorism—also called
Islamic radicalism by some—US politicians such as former speaker of
the house Newt Gingrich and Republican presidential candidate Donald
Trump abandoned Eisenhower's religious bargain. For them, the enemy
was not someone who happened to be Muslim, but instead, it was radical
Islamic religion itself. Therefore, defeating the enemy meant protecting
the borders of the country from the presence of what Trump considered to
be a foreign and dangerous ideology. One way to do that was to effectively
ban Muslims from visiting or immigrating to the United States through
"extreme vetting."

But when Trump attacked the family of a fallen soldier, and did so in a
personal way, he fell into the trap that Clinton's campaign had set for him.
This attack went too far for many fellow Republicans. Many of them spoke
out against Trump or offered words of sympathy and appreciation for the
sacrifice of the Khan family.

What was little noticed at the time was that most Muslims disagreed
heartily with Clinton's foreign policy positions toward various countries
with Muslim-majority populations. As a US senator and then as secretary
of state, Clinton had been a voice for aggressive military intervention in
the Muslim world. She supported the 2003 war in Iraq, a war that resulted
in the deaths of hundreds of thousands of Muslims. As secretary of state,
she urged President Barack Obama to join with NATO in toppling Libyan
leader Muammar Qaddafi, and she forcefully argued for more US involvement in the Syrian civil war. Her hawkish positions were opposed by the
vast majority of Muslims both at home and abroad.

But for Clinton, one issue had nothing to do with the other. The fallen
Muslim American soldier was a Muslim who helped protect America. He
was not the same as those foreign Muslims who had been killed in the
Iraq and Afghanistan wars. He was an American. It was such a powerful
symbol that it had already been used in another presidential election after
9/11—the election of Barack Hussein Obama in 2008.

CORPORAL KAREEM KHAN AND THE ELECTION OF 2008

Cpl. Kareem Rashad Sultan Khan—no relation to Humayun Khan—grew up in Manahawkin, New Jersey. His dad, Feroze Khan, said he was a "total goofball." Khan was known, for example, to consume only the orange-flavored Starburst candies, leaving the rest for others to eat. He went to Disney World on an annual basis, and his father's home became a shrine to Disney characters. The split-level house featured "a wall hanging of Cinderella, figurines of Mickey Mouse, and Disney-themed snow globes."[10] Khan was a Dallas Cowboys fan and a lover of video games—he would sit on the living room floor and play with his stepsister, Aliya, for hours. But Khan also had a serious side. When al-Qaeda attacked the World Trade Center on 9/11, he was determined to show the world that "not all Muslims were fanatics and that many, like him, were willing to lay down their lives for their country."[11] He signed up for the Air Force Junior ROTC as a high school freshman, and after graduating from Southern Regional High School in 2005, he enlisted in the US Army.

Khan attended basic training at Fort Benning, Georgia, and was assigned to the First Battalion, Twenty-Third Infantry Regiment, Third Brigade, Second Infantry Division, known as the "Stryker Brigade Combat Team." He spent a few months at the team's home base, Fort Lewis, Washington, and then shipped out to Iraq. Specialist Khan's emails to his family were upbeat. He believed in the mission. Even his choice of Hollywood movies indicated as much. He loved watching *Saving Private Ryan* and *Letters from Iwo Jima.* He sent photographs of himself playing soccer with Iraqi kids. One boy took a special liking to him and followed him around wherever he went.[12]

The Stryker Brigade Combat Team finished its assignment in Iraq, but their tour was extended as part of the surge to battle the Iraqi rebellion. On August 6, 2007, Khan was in Baqubah, a city northeast of the capital, Baghdad. He was clearing a house, which meant that he was looking for insurgents. A bomb went off, killing him and three other soldiers.

Khan was buried at Arlington National Cemetery and posthumously promoted to corporal. This twenty-year-old was given both a Bronze Star and a Purple Heart.[13]

The story of Cpl. Kareem Khan, like that of Capt. Humayun Khan, may have been known only to a few if it were not for former secretary of state and retired chairman of the joint chiefs of staff Gen. Colin Powell. Two weeks before the presidential election of 2008, Powell, who had served as secretary of state under Republican President George W. Bush, endorsed Democrat Barack Obama for president. He went on the NBC program *Meet the Press* to do so. Powell explained he was disturbed by the anti-Muslim rhetoric in his own political party. He was troubled that some people were "accusing" Obama of being a Muslim.

"What if he is?" the general asked, rhetorically. "Is there something wrong with being a Muslim in this country? The answer is 'No, that's not America.' Is there something wrong with some seven-year-old Muslim American kid believing that he or she could be president?"

Where was all this passion coming from?

"I feel strongly about this particular point because of a picture I saw in a magazine," explained Powell. That picture, taken by the photographer Platon, was, in Powell's words, "of a mother in Arlington Cemetery. And she had her head on the headstone of her son's grave. . . . He was twenty years old. And then at the very top of the headstone, it didn't have a Christian cross. It didn't have a Star of David. It had a crescent and a star of the Islamic faith. And his name was Karim Rashad Sultan Khan. And he was an American."[14]

Platon remembered taking the photograph. "One day I saw this lady, and every day she goes to his son's grave. She sits in front of her son's grave and reads to him." Platon asked her if he could take her picture. "She took the book that she was reading and placed it at the base of the headstone, and got behind the stone and cuddled it as if she was embracing her son."[15]

The woman was Khan's mother, Elsheba Khan. She is depicted with her eyes closed. Her head is resting on her left arm, which is draped gently across the top of the gravestone. Her right arm is extended down the right side of the marker, as she embraces her son's gravestone. The image is reminiscent, as one scholar points out, of the Pietà, Michelangelo's sculpture located in St. Peter's Basilica that depicts Mary, the mother of Jesus, embracing her dead son.[16]

Like Mary, Khan's mother gave up her son for a purpose much larger than herself. She sacrificed her son for the nation. And Powell ensured that the sacrifice of this young man, twenty years old, would not be in vain but would be remembered as giving life to something superhuman, a better love of America and its ideals.

As a child who grew up in the shadow of the fallen towers of the World Trade Center, Khan was so deeply shaped by the idea of proving his patriotism that he named it as his reason for joining the military. Even though he had grown up in the United States, even though he was quintessentially

Kareem Khan's gravesite at Arlington National Cemetery became a symbol in national conversations leading up the 2008 US presidential election. (Photo courtesy of Arlington National Cemetery.)

American, the ghost of 9/11 was so powerful that it needed to be exorcised with his blood.

No one should doubt Khan's sincerity. Or his sacrifice. Or his free will. But should Muslim youth have to carry the burden of proving their religious community's loyalty to the United States?

At the heart of the story of these two fallen soldiers, Cpl. Kareem Khan and Capt. Humayun Khan, is the question of whether Muslim armed service members and Muslim Americans more generally are doomed and destined to play symbolic roles over which they may have limited control. No matter how one answers that question, the sacrifice of Muslims serving in the US military should at the very least inspire us all to know them better. If Americans who happen to be Muslim are to become less symbolic and more real, their public image needs to become less idealized and more complex—not the subject of only romantic patriotism or ugly racism but also of something else, something more ordinary. Understanding the long history of their military service, its triumphs and its everyday, mundane reality—and yes, its symbolic value—is a necessary step in coming to appreciate Muslim American armed service members and Muslim Americans as a whole as human. Just human.

Notes

1. The account above is based on Missy Ryan, "Capt. Humayun Khan, Whose Grieving Parents Have Been Criticized by Trump, Was 'a Soldier's Officer,'" *Washington Post*, August 2, 2016; and Dana J. H. Pitard, "I Was Capt. Khan's Commander in Iraq," *Washington Post*, August 3, 2016.

2. Around half a billion people, about 30 percent of all Muslims in the world, live in South Asia. "10 Countries with the Largest Muslim Populations, 2010 and 2050," Pew Research Center, April 2, 2015, http://www.pewforum.org/2015/04/02 /muslims/pf_15-04-02_projectionstables74/.

3. Michele Clock, "A 'Peacemaker' Is Laid to Rest: Muslim Soldier From Prince William Tried to Improve Relations in Iraq," *Washington Post*, June 16, 2004, as reproduced in "Humayun Saqib Muazzam Khan," Arlington National Cemetery, http://www.arlingtoncemetery.net/hsmkhan.htm.

4. "Who Was Capt Humayun Khan?" *BBC News*, August 1, 2016, http://www .bbc.com/news/election-us-2016-36945318.

5. Reporting on the love story of Khan and Auer is by N. R. Kleinfield, Richard A. Oppel Jr., and Melissa Eddy, "Moment in Convention Glare Shakes Up Khans' American Life," *New York Times*, August 5, 2016.

6. Khizr Khan, "Speech to the 2016 Democratic National Convention," ABC News, August 1, 2016, http://abcnews.go.com/Politics/full-text-khizr-khans-speech -2016-democratic-national/story?id=41043609.

7. Pitard, "I Was Capt. Khan's Commander in Iraq."

8. Ghazala Khan, "Trump Criticized My Silence. He Knows Nothing About Me," *Washington Post*, July 31, 2016.

9. Dwight D. Eisenhower, "1957 Speech at Islamic Center of Washington," IIP Digital, June 28, 1957, http://iipdigital.usembassy.gov/st/english/texttrans/2007/06 /20070626154822lnkaiso.6946985.html#axzz4IcvFMoOf.

10. Shruti L. Mathur, "Blast Kills Jersey Shore GI," *South Jersey Courier Post*, August 10, 2007, as reproduced in "Kareem Rashad Sultan Khan," Arlington National Cemetery Website, http://www.arlingtoncemetery.net/krkhan.htm.

11. Shruti L. Mathur, "Blast Kills Jersey Shore GI," *South Jersey Courier Post*, August 10, 2007, as reproduced in "Kareem Rashad Sultan Khan," Arlington National Cemetery Website, http://www.arlingtoncemetery.net/krkhan.htm.

12. Maryann Spoto and Wayne Woolley, "Ocean GI Is State's 80th Casualty," *New Jersey Star-Ledger*, August 10, 2007, as reproduced in http://blog.nj.com /njwardead/2007/08/army_spc_kareem_r_khan_august.html.

13. Ibid.

14. *"Meet the Press* Transcript for Oct. 19, 2008," *NBC News*, October 19, 2008, http://www.nbcnews.com/id/27266223/#.V7tAnWUUgkc.

15. Video with Platon in "Why Colin Powell's Emotional Obama Endorsement Is Going Viral Again," *Huffington Post*, August 5, 2016, http://www.huffingtonpost .com/entry/colin-powell-khan-photograph_us_57a3aebce4b021fd98781442.

16. Ji-Young Um, "Citizen and Terrorist, Citizen as Terrorist," *Postmodern Culture* 22, no. 3 (May 2012): https://muse.jhu.edu/.

TWO

THE LONG HISTORY OF MUSLIM AMERICAN WARRIORS: FROM THE REVOLUTION TO WORLD WAR II

DURING THE AMERICAN REVOLUTION, men such as Bampett Muhamed, Joseph Benenhaley (perhaps Yusuf Ben Ali), Francis and Joseph Saba, and Peter Salem fought for the thirteen colonies and, starting in 1776, the young United States of America. Salem fired the shot that killed British Maj. Pitcairn at the Battle of Bunker Hill, known as one of the first engagements of the American Revolution. Muhamed served in Virginia. Benenhaley, said to be born in the Ottoman Empire, was a scout for Gen. Thomas Sumter.[1]

Some of these men may have come from a Muslim background, but without additional research, it remains hard to know for certain. Of all the wars in which Muslims have fought for the United States, the Revolutionary War (1775–1783) is the most difficult to document. But surely Muslims were involved. Tens of thousands of enslaved African Muslims arrived in the United States in the 1700s.[2] They included a man of Hausa heritage named Sambo, who was enslaved by Gen. George Washington and worked on Mount Vernon, the general's Virginia plantation.[3]

By the War of 1812, when the British attempted to recapture their lost North American possessions, there is no doubt that Muslims were actively defending the United States. In 1813, Bilali Mahomet led an informal militia of eighty other slaves armed with muskets ready to defend Sapelo Island, Georgia, from British invasion. Mahomet, born in the West African country of Futa Jalon, was a literate, observant Muslim, trained in Sharia, or Islamic law and ethics. Mahomet never saw action, perhaps because the

British had gotten wind of the armed men on Sapelo. Plantation and slave owner Thomas Spaulding trusted Mahomet's considerable talents as an overseer. He must have. Georgia was the only colony that banned African Americans from fighting in the American Revolution, and just down the way at St. Simons Island, many enslaved people had run away to the British, who offered freedom to enslaved African Americans. No one did so on Mahomet's watch.[4]

For centuries now, Muslim Americans, both slave and free, have taken up arms to defend the United States. Some stories of their military service are typical—like when thousands of Muslims served on the front lines of World War I and World War II. But at least one tale of their military service is—it must be said—exotic.

WESTWARD EXPANSION: THE CAMEL CORPS

Perhaps the most unusual story of Muslim American military history is that of Hadji Ali, the Muslim assigned to help the US Army develop camel caravans as a mode of shipping in the American Southwest. Born to a Greek mother and an Arab father around 1828, the man who came to be known as "Hi Jolly" could scarcely have guessed that his memory would be invoked in a much-recorded folk song, an annual festival in Arizona, and educational camel tours in Texas state parks.

In 1855, Secretary of War Jefferson Davis, who would later become president of the Confederacy, procured $30,000 from the US Congress to develop camels as military transport. The United States had only recently come into possession of what used to be Mexican territory thanks to its victory in the Mexican-American War of 1846. Easterners surged west in 1849 after gold was discovered in California. Camels, it was thought, would be able to traverse the arid, rugged terrain with ease.

Maj. Henry C. Wayne traveled to various ports on the Mediterranean to study and purchase the camels. "Nine dromedaries, or runners, 23 camels of burden, and 1 calf" were loaded onto the *Supply* under the command of then Lt. David Dixon Porter. They came into port in 1856 in Indianola, Texas. More camels would arrive the next year, and the experiment was ready to go.

To give the experiment its best chance at success, the army thought to hire an expert camel driver. This is how Ali came to America.

Ali, who also arrived in Texas in 1856, helped ready "Uncle Sam's Camels" for their long journey. In addition to the camels, the caravan was composed of 56 men, 350 sheep, and 8 covered wagons—pulled by mules,

Hadji Ali was recruited from the Middle East as part of the US Army's Camel Corps. (1880; University of North Texas Libraries, The Portal to Texas History, crediting Marfa Public Library.)

not camels. The camels carried hundreds of pounds of water and other supplies and covered over twenty-five miles a day. Leaving San Antonio, Texas, on June 25, 1857, the caravan traveled to New Mexico and Arizona. On October 18, they arrived at the Colorado River. By November, they had made it to Fort Tejon, north of Los Angeles.

Lt. Edward F. Beale, the naval officer in charge of the expedition, wrote that his "admiration for the camels increases daily." John Floyd, the new secretary of war under President James Buchanan, declared the camel experiment a success and asked Congress to authorize the purchase of one thousand more animals. When he received nothing in reply, he asked again in 1859. In December 1860, Secretary Floyd was still a believer in the future of the Camel Corps.

But when President Abraham Lincoln took office in 1861, the new secretary of war, Edwin Stanton, had little time for the dromedaries. He had to fight the Civil War. Plus, not all service members were as admiring of the camels as Beale.

Ali was stuck in California with the camels, and Beale said his men were bored. In 1863, the War Department ordered that the camels be sold. The camel experiment was over, and Ali was left without a job.[5]

There are some reports that he prospected for gold. He also worked off and on as a scout for the army in Arizona. An 1870 report from Fort Mc-Dowell indicates that he was employed as a civilian pack master, earning $100 per month.[6] But his work with the US military was unsteady.

In 1880, when he became a naturalized US citizen in Tucson, Arizona, he took the name Philip Tedro. Some reports indicate that perhaps his mother had been Greek and Tedro had been his birth name. He married a woman named Gertruda Serna and had two daughters. But Tedro spent long periods of time away from his family, perhaps abandoning them when he moved outside of Quartzsite, Arizona. He died broke in 1902.[7]

But he was not forgotten. The legend of Hi Jolly only grew over the years. In 1935, the Arizona Highway Department, evidently playing on the exotic legend, erected a pyramid-shaped marker over his tomb. At the top of the memorial stands a one-humped camel. The plaque on the memorial declares the spot to be the "last camp of Hi Jolly . . . Camel driver—packer scout—over thirty years a faithful aid to the U.S. government."[8]

The story of the Camel Corps and Hi Jolly became part of US popular culture, the subject of children's books, radio dramas, and films such as *Southwest Passage* (1954) and *Hawmps* (1976). The folk song "Hi Jolly, The Camel Driver" has been recorded by the New Christy Minstrels (1962), the Travelers 3 (1962), the Canadiana Folksingers (1964), the Merrymen (1993), and the River City Ramblers (2001). The song, written by Randy Sparks, includes the idea that Hi Jolly's ghost still haunts the desert: "Old timers down in Arizona tell you that it's true / That you can see Hi Jolly's ghost a-ridin' still / When the desert moon is bright, he comes ridin' into sight / Drivin' four and twenty camels over the hill."[9]

Today you can also try to imagine what it was like to be Hi Jolly by joining a Big Bend Camel Trek in some of the same territory that he originally traversed. A three-day tour by the Texas Camel Corps uses "ranch roads, cattle trails, creek beds, and mountain passes" outside of the old Fort Davis in the Big Bend region of Texas in order to teach customers about the use of the camel in the US Southwest.

The story of the real Tedro is in many ways a sad one, but his legend has become something else altogether. It is also unusual. Until recently, the military service of Muslims has attracted little attention. This includes the service of hundreds of Muslims during the US Civil War (1861–1865), when President Abraham Lincoln refused to recognize the decision of the Confederate States of America to withdraw from the United States. This war, fought over the legality of human slavery, resulted in over half a million deaths—perhaps as many as 750,000. It remains a central element of American identity, and Muslims were part of it.

The Civil War and the Sojourns of Sergeant Said

Sgt. Nicholas Said was surely one of the most remarkably well-traveled, cosmopolitan soldiers to fight in the US Civil War. In fact, Said was one of the most incredible travelers of the entire nineteenth century. In one of his service records, his place of birth was listed as Detroit.[10] But Detroit could not have been farther from where he was actually born.

Mohammed Ali ben Said (ca. 1831–1882), later called Nicholas, came from the Central African state of Bornu, located around Lake Chad. He was one of nineteen children, and according to his own account in an 1873 autobiography, his mother had trouble keeping him at home from an early age. His hunts for gazelles and guinea fowl would take him miles away from the city of his birth. Young Said loved to play in the forest. "The forests of Bornu," he wrote, "are full of all kinds of wild beasts, such as lions, panthers, yenas or hyenas, jackals, elephants, rhinoceroses, tigers, and a great many more less harmful, but not less troublesome creatures."[11]

Said was less fond of his country's politics. He criticized unnecessary violence and the domination of one social group over another based on their ethnicity and religion. When his father was killed in war during Said's adolescence, he was cared for by a Muslim scholar, and only then did he become a practitioner of Islam.

More tragedy befell the young man. He was captured in a raid by the Tuaregs and sold into slavery. His owner, Abd El-Kader, took him north across the Sahara. He was sold again to a Turkish official of the Ottoman Empire. Then he was sold a third time and sent to Tripoli, located in contemporary Libya. This new master, Hajj Dawud, took him on the hajj, the

Islamic pilgrimage to Mecca, and to the shrine of the Prophet Muhammad in Medina, also located in western Arabia. When they returned, Said was sent to Izmir, Turkey, to be sold once again.

Eventually, Said became the slave of a Russian prince, Mentchikoff, and lived in a palace in Odessa, located on the Black Sea. By now, Said could speak Arabic, Turkish, and Russian, in addition to his native language. Prince Mentchikoff was himself kind, but his servants were brutal, and Said asked to serve another master. Thus he became the servant of Prince Nicholas Vassilievitch Troubetzkoy in St. Petersburg.

Prince Troubetzkoy made Said learn French and forced him to convert to Christianity, which is when Mohammed Ali ben became Nicholas. Said was a baptized Christian, but how much he identified with his new religion is uncertain. Said dubbed his baptism a "performance" and made fun of the religious devotions of his master: "Whenever he went to prayers, he made me stand before him . . . and imitate every action of his, such as kneeling, bowing, making the sign of the cross." Said noted, "I used to enjoy myself hugely, cutting capers and going through all sorts of pantomimic performances when he thought I was acting in a very devotional manner." When the prince caught him having fun, he gave Said a "*striking* reminder of what was decent and respectful on such solemn occasions, by administering to my ears a good boxing and depriving me of my dinner." The prince's Christianity was not to be mocked, and violence and deprivation were supposed to teach Said his lesson.

Later, when the priest who baptized Said made him kneel for hours in repentant repose, Said used a sarcastic tone to describe what happened:

> I found myself in a beautiful chapel, handsomely paved with marble of different colors. He caused me to kneel before an immense *tableau* of the Saviour for hours, asking pardons for my past sins. As the marble was harder than my knees, I was in perfect agony during the greater portion of the time, and became so enraged with the *papa*, that I fear I committed more sins during that space of time than I had done in days before. In fact, I am not sure but that a few ungainly Mohammedan [Muslim] asperities of language bubbled up to my lips. But I managed to get through without any overt act of rebellion.

Even after converting to Christianity, Said continued to use Arabic-Islamic insults to express some of his most basic feelings about being punished. Perhaps his sarcasm was merely a critique of Orthodox Christianity's lush rituals. He may not have felt the same way about Protestantism.

Sgt. Nicholas Said served in the Fifty-Fifth (Colored) Infantry Regiment from Massachusetts during the US Civil War. (Unidentified photographer, circa 1863–1866, Wolcott family Civil War carte de visite album, Massachusetts Historical Society.)

But maybe he was cynical about all religion, whether Islamic or Christian. Said's religious views are an important reminder that Muslim members of the armed services may be shaped by their Muslim backgrounds, but they do not see their religious heritage in the same light. They may not practice Islamic religion at all. It simply depends on the service member.

After his baptism, Said traveled with the prince to Moscow, Warsaw, Vienna, Dresden, Munich—which had "excellent Bavarian beer"—and to Salzburg, Baden-Baden, Milan, Genoa, Pisa, Florence, Rome, Paris, and London. It was a grand tour. And then, Said asked the prince if he could visit his homeland. The prince consented, but Said decided instead to accept the offer of one De Sanddrost I. J. Rochussen of Suriname to become his servant during a tour of the Americas.

Said set sail on the *Bohemian* to Portland, Maine, stopping for a brief time in Boston and New York before taking the *Karnak* to the Bahamas. They visited Haiti together and then returned from New York. From there, they traveled to several Canadian cities, landing in the town of Aylmer.

Then, tragedy struck again. Rochussen borrowed £300 from Said and absconded with the money.

Said had to start all over again. He went to Detroit in 1862, and then on June 22, 1863, he enlisted in the Union Army. During the Civil War, 179,000 African American soldiers and 19,000 sailors served on the Union side.[12] Said joined the Fifty-Fifth Massachusetts (Colored) Infantry Regiment.[13] This was the sister unit of the Fifty-Fourth Massachusetts Infantry, which famously charged Fort Wagner in 1863—an event later made into the movie *Glory*.

It is unclear if other Muslims or those from a Muslim background served in the Fifty-Fourth or Fifty-Fifth during the war, but the presence of Muslim names on both sides of the war suggests there were perhaps hundreds of troops who served for either the Confederacy or the Union. The Muslim presence in the 1800s was undeniable. Muslims were among the most well-known African Americans in the first half of the 1800s. These figures included Abdul Rahman Ibrahima, who visited John Quincy Adams at the White House; Yarrow Mamout, who sat for a portrait by the famed painter Charles Willson Peale; and Omar Said, who penned the first Arabic-language autobiography in the United States in 1831.[14]

Independent scholar Amir Muhammad has counted at least 292 Muslim-sounding last names in both the Confederate and Union armies.[15] These include 1st Sgt. Max Hassan of Providence, Rhode Island, who served in the Fourteenth Heavy Artillery Regiment, which became part of the Eleventh Heavy Artillery. His service record lists him as having been born in "Africa."[16]

There is also the curious case of Ali ben Moussa, or Ali, son of Musa. Born in Algeria, he enlisted with the Union Army in 1863 and went south with the Fifth Rhode Island Heavy Artillery. Then, that same year, he apparently deserted—it's not clear why—and joined Capt. Brander's Light Artillery in the Confederate Army.[17]

According to Nicholas Said's service record, in October 1863 he became the sergeant "on duty on Long Island [South Carolina] in charge of squad," or Company J of the Fifty-Fifth Massachusetts Infantry. In May 1864, Said is recorded as being absent from his duty at headquarters. He was then referred to in the record as "Private Said," indicating that he may have received a demotion from sergeant. No reason is given for his absence, but it would be wrong to assume that he was simply derelict in his duty. African American soldiers were often the victims of anti-black racism inside the Union Army, and in South Carolina, military governor

Gen. Rufus Saxton was widely known for his blatant anti-black attitudes. Said weathered whatever challenges he faced and eventually found an edifying post. After being detailed on September 1, 1864, to serve as a clerk in the adjutant's office, he soon received another special order dated November 1, 1864, for daily duty at the regimental hospital.[18]

Said was detailed to assist Dr. Burt Green Wilder, the white Boston surgeon and Harvard-trained anatomist who volunteered to serve in the Fifty-Fifth Infantry. In his diary, Wilder described Said as a talented and intellectually curious soldier. "I have the advantage of the clerical aid of Nicholas Said, the native African, who is very intelligent and writes an excellent hand," he wrote on Monday, April 24, 1865. "By the way," he noted the next day, Said "is very philosophical in his mind and interested in unusual things, religious problems, etc." On April 30, he wrote that Said had now read half of Emanuel Swedenborg's *Divine Love and Wisdom*.[19] Swedenborg was a scientist and Christian theologian who wrote prolifically in order to reform Christianity based on his divine visions. What Said thought of Swedenborg is unclear, but it is perhaps unsurprising that this intellectual polyglot was fascinated with theology.

The war ended on May 9, 1865, and Said mustered out on August 29, 1865, at Charleston, South Carolina.[20] According to his autobiography, he left Charleston in 1870 and went on to travel, speak, write, and teach, landing for a time in Bladon Springs, Alabama. "My honest desire," he wrote in the conclusion to his autobiography, "is to render myself useful to my race." Said's entire memoir is unsparing in its criticism of those with power and wealth who abuse others in the name of religion, race, or some other form of privilege. "To me," he concluded, "it is impossible to conceive how a human being can be happy through any other channel, than to do as much good as possible to his fellow-man in this world."

Said's criticisms of the powerful people's sometimes callous disregard for those less fortunate were prescient as the country moved from the Civil War and Reconstruction to a historical period dubbed the "Gilded Age" by author Mark Twain. Once Reconstruction ended in 1877 and federal troops departed from the former Confederacy, the US military focused its attention elsewhere. The US Army was ordered to keep Native Americans on their reservations and to punish those who refused to submit to the US takeover of their lands. In 1893, the military also conquered Queen Lili'uokalani of Hawaii. In 1898, the military fought the Spanish American war, which led to more than a decade of fighting in the Philippines, many of whose inhabitants resisted US conquest. Muslim service in the military during this era is a story that will have to wait for another telling. Instead, we turn to World War I (1913–1917), also known as the Great War, which pitted Germany, the Austro-Hungarian Empire, and the Ottoman Empire against the British Empire, France, the Russian Empire, and eventually, the United States. Millions of Muslims fought on both sides of World War I, and thousands served in the American Expeditionary Forces (AEF).

World War I: From the Prairie to the Argonne Forest

Pvt. Omer Otmen's Company K was ordered to join the first wave of the 360th Infantry's attack against German forces, including the division called the "Kaiser's favorites."[21] This was part of the Meuse-Argonne Offensive, the AEF's most important campaign in World War I. Gen. John J. "Black Jack" Pershing led over a million troops in the battle that finally brought the "war to end all wars" to a conclusion. The price in blood and treasure would be high—over 26,000 killed and almost 96,000 wounded.

On an ominous Halloween night in 1918, the German army waited in a system of trenches designed to stop the advance of Otmen's company. Had it not been for the war, this place would have been lovely. Otmen likely saw a gentle ridge covered with trees rising in front of him, and if had he been able to see beyond that, he would have gazed on an undulating topography of ridges and valleys that descended toward the Meuse River.

The Americans were supposed to begin bombing German positions at 3:30 in the morning. But the Germans discovered their presence beforehand, and by the midnight hour, they directed massive artillery fire toward the American side. The Americans had no shelter, no cover. For Otmen and his fellow soldiers, the Halloween night sky was ignited by thermite bombs in what was described as a horrifying rain of fire. Thirty-six soldiers were injured or killed, and the German forces even hit a US command post.

The US assault finally began on schedule. After bombing the German positions for two hours, Otmen's second platoon advanced toward the German lines, overwhelming the Germans in their trenches. They captured seventy men along with their machine guns and other military equipment. Later, the commanding general of the Ninetieth Division cited Otmen by name for his bravery.

By the next day, the 360th Infantry had won this small plot of land and was ready to continue the advance. The regiment suffered heavy casualties over the next several days, but on November 11, the armistice was declared

Kassam Rameden, as he is listed on his military registration, emigrated from Syria to the American West, and served, like Otmen, in the Meuse-Argonne Offensive during World War I. (National Archives.)[22]

and the fighting stopped. Company K and others now set their sights both on maintaining order as German troops withdrew from Belgium and, eventually, on occupying Germany itself.

Since Company K was staying put for a few months, a semblance of regular life was established. Members of the Young Men's Christian Association (YMCA) tended to the spiritual care of the troops, as did three different chaplains. Over seven hundred people attended regular Sunday Christian services.

The regiment took a survey of its own religious composition. Most were Christians of one kind or another. There were two Jewish officers and eighteen Jewish soldiers, but no Muslims. How was this possible? Had Otmen converted to another religion? Did he simply stop practicing religion altogether? Perhaps he was one of 359 men to say that he had no religious preference. It was not unusual for Muslims to avoid discussing their religious identity at this time.

More likely than not, Otmen's religious identity was simply unknown to his fellow soldiers. America's enemies in World War I included Germany, the Austro-Hungarian Empire, and the Ottoman Empire, the birthplace of Otmen. Some Muslims, such as Mohammed Mostfa, had been discharged from the US Army "by reason of being an alien enemy." But these Muslim soldiers did not sign on to defend the Muslim empire in which they were born. They came to fight for their new country, the United States.

According to the *Official Roster of North Dakota Soldiers, Sailors, and Marines*, Otmen was a twenty-nine-year-old farmer when he signed up for military service in Ashley, North Dakota, on June 5, 1917. By April 1918, he was officially inducted into the army and sent to Camp Dodge in Iowa. In June, he was sent to the front, and by 1919, he was discharged.[23]

The story of Otmen may seem rare. It was not. According to the US War Department, 13,965 Syrian Americans, or 7 percent of the total Syrian American population, served in uniform during World War I. [24]

As Arab Americans, they shared, more or less, a common language—Arabic—and held in common many cultural traditions. But they subscribed to an incredibly diverse set of religious traditions. The majority of them were Christian, members of Maronite, Melkite, Roman Catholic, Orthodox, or other Christian sects. Some were Druze, members of an Eastern Mediterranean religious group with a heritage that dates from the eleventh century. Still others were Muslims, and these Muslims were from the Sunni sect of Islam, by far the largest, and the Shia sect. Though sharing much in common, Sunni and Shia Muslims divided, among other reasons, over a disagreement about who was best qualified to lead Muslims after the death of the Prophet Muhammad. The Sunnis determined the leader through the consensus of tribal leaders; the Shia thought that members of the Prophet's family should lead the community.[25]

Perhaps 10 percent of the Syrian Americans in uniform were Sunni or Shia Muslims. They were not the only Muslim Americans to serve; other Muslims registered with draft came from Bengali, Punjabi, Bosnian, Tatar, and other backgrounds.[26] But Syrian Muslims were probably the largest group of Muslim American military members in the Great War.

Syrian Americans settled all over the United States but were concentrated on the East Coast and in the Midwest, especially in cities such as Detroit and Chicago. Otmen lived in what turned out to be a rural center of Syrian American Muslim life—North Dakota. North Dakota's Syrian community was more Muslim than the rest of the country. Around one third of North Dakota's Syrians came from a Muslim background.[27]

In 1920, Muslims in the town of Ross, North Dakota, established an Islamic cemetery. Some veterans would eventually be buried there, including World War I veteran Alex Asmal of the 158th Infantry, Fortieth Division, who died in 1941.[28]

The headstone application for deceased World War I veteran Alex Asmal, filed in 1942, contained a request for a "Mahommedan" or Muslim emblem. (National Archives.)[29]

In 1929, local residents started to build their own mosque for community members, both Sunni and Shia. It was a simple post-and-beam structure, a sunken building that barely rose above the ground. It was made for the harsh winters of North Dakota, where one can barely imagine how cold the January floor must have felt when prostrating one's body in prayer toward Mecca.[30]

Muslims did not seek religious sanctuary in North Dakota. They came for the American dream. Some of them were peddlers, and others sought work as farm hands. Many hoped for the 160 acres of land that they might be granted for free by the federal Homestead Act. But by the 1930s, in the midst of the Great Depression, a collapsed farm economy, and a horrible drought, many of these sodbusters lamented their chosen profession.[31] Yet they did not regret their decision to immigrate to the United States, and the World War I veterans among them remained proud of their service in the war. One of them was Kassam Rameden (1892–1964), also known as Kassen "Sam" Rameden, who, like Otmen, served in Europe during the war.

Rameden was born on a five- to six-acre hilly farm not far from the city of Damascus, Syria. He lived with his family in a two-story stone house. Unlike North Dakota, Rameden said his region of Syria was warm, and even when the countryside was blanketed in winter by two or three feet of snow, "it would all disappear in a day or two."[32]

His Syrian family attended daily worship services at the local mosque. "The congregation would kneel," he said, "with their heads bowed to the floor and pray, while the preacher chanted hymns," likely meaning that he chanted the prescribed words for the five daily prayers called *salat* and perhaps words of praise for God and God's prophets. "Our Sabbath came on Friday instead of Sunday," Rameden explained, referring to the fact that congregational prayers are required on Friday at midday.

Rameden's family paid a local Islamic scholar to teach him how to read and write in Arabic. They were only able to send him to school for a year. Most of the time, Rameden was busy working in his family's fields, using oxen to plow the ground and broadcasting their grain and vegetable seeds by hand. They harvested grain with a scythe or cradle, bundled the grain up with ropes, balanced the bundles on the sides of donkeys, and sent them to town.

"It was not all work," remembered Rameden. Village life included parties, communal meals, weddings, horse races, and games.

But from the time he was a boy, Rameden had heard his elders talk about "wonderful America, where opportunity was open to all, and where there was more freedom for everyone." In addition to the American dream, which pulled Rameden toward US shores, he left because he worried he would soon be conscripted into the Ottoman army.

So, Rameden and an older brother saved up enough money and purchased passage to America. He sailed from the city of Beirut in 1911. Disembarking in New York, he went to Sioux City, Iowa, where he worked at a packing plant for forty-two cents an hour. Rameden traveled from there to North Dakota and then Montana, and finally in 1917, he joined the US Army.

In 1918, Rameden applied to become a US citizen when he was stationed at Camp Kearny in San Diego County, California. He joined the 157th Infantry and, like Otmen, served in the Meuse-Argonne Offensive. "I was glad to fight over there," he remembered later, "because we were told it was to 'make the world safe for democracy.'"

In 1919, Rameden was discharged from the army, and in 1921, he married Mary Bella Lynch, an American of Irish descent. They had six children, and his son, Kassen Jr., would later serve in the Korean War.

The Immigration Act of 1924 severely curtailed immigration from all countries except those in northwestern Europe. But the children of immigrants who arrived before World War I once again enlisted in large numbers during World War II (1939–1945), in which over a hundred million people fought either for the Allied powers of the Soviet Union, Great Britain, and the United States or for the Axis powers of Germany, Japan, and Italy. Thousands of Muslim Americans served in a conflict that would become the deadliest in the history of humankind.

WORLD WAR II

It must have felt like walking the plank, except in something like forty-two degrees below zero, thousands of feet high, and accompanied by the sounds of German anti-aircraft artillery, whose only purpose was to take you out of the sky.

Sgt. John Ramsey Omar (1924–2007) was a flight engineer and turret gunner on an aircraft called the B-24 Liberator. His plane was nicknamed "She's Our Gal." As the crew prepared to drop thousands of pounds of bombs on Magdeburg, Germany, one of their engines was hit and a rudder cable was severed.

The bomb bay doors would not open. The crew would not be able to complete its mission.

Omar realized he was going to have to open the bomb bay doors manually. He disconnected his flight suit and made his way along the nine-inch-wide catwalk that ran from the cockpit to the waste door. Omar grasped ahold of the struts, which rose vertically on both sides of the narrow catwalk. He could see the earth below, and one misstep would mean certain death. Putting his hands on the cranks, he got the bomb bay doors open.

Then, he caught some shrapnel in his right foot.

Later, Omar would be awarded a Purple Heart, but there was no time to think about awards right now. He was injured, and there was more work to be done. Omar had to repair the severed rudder cable so they could turn the plane around. There was no time to spare. Without one of their engines, they were losing altitude. And they were running out of fuel too.

They made a successful emergency landing in a little Belgian field, despite the fact that their fuselage had sustained forty-four hits.

Omar became severely ill, and an ambulance transported him to a hospital in Antwerp, Belgium. Diagnosed with double pneumonia, he fell into a coma. He awoke a week later to the sound of German bombs, some of which destroyed parts of the hospital.

After a forty-one-day stay, Omar was released and told to return to his base. Since he had no idea how to get there, he asked a couple of military police officers (MPs) for help. They gave him a train ticket to Brussels, and

John Omar daringly cranked open the bomb doors of a B-24 Liberator
by hand during a bombing run over Nazi Germany. (US Air Force photo
[Public Domain] via Wikimedia Commons.)

from there he wandered around the city looking for the displaced persons
center.

When he arrived, Omar was told he had been listed as missing in action, and before letting him return to his base in England, military officials
called his commander to confirm his identity.

Once he fully recovered, Omar flew more missions out of his home
base in Pickenham Airfield in Norfolk, England. As a member of 491st
Bomb Group of the Eighth Air Force, US Army Air Corps, Omar flew a
total of twenty-nine missions during the war.

During the Battle of the Bulge (1944–1945), a German offensive in
which approximately one hundred thousand US military personnel were

killed or injured, Omar had another close call. Shortly after takeoff in the middle of a massive snow storm, his plane crashed. Eleven of the plane's five-hundred-pound bombs fell on the ground far enough away from the plane, but one hurled itself through the cockpit bulkhead just inches from Omar's back. Omar assisted the pilot as they both ran away from what they feared would be an explosion.[33]

Omar survived, and he was discharged in 1945. Soon after coming home from the war, Omar married Mary Awad. He opened Omar's Auto Electric Service and worked there for five decades. Omar was also a member of the Islamic Center of New England, located in Sharon, Massachusetts. When he died, his obituary referred to him as "Haj" John Omar, an honorific title given to those who travel to Mecca to perform the annual pilgrimage.[34]

Omar was one of perhaps fifteen thousand Arab American men and women to serve in World War II. They went to Europe to fight the Nazi regime and the Italian army, and they served in the Pacific theater, fighting the Empire of Japan. As in World War I, most of these Arab service members were from Lebanese and Syrian backgrounds, and perhaps 10 percent of them were Muslim. Many of the females who volunteered did so as nurses, although women also served in other roles, including the Women Airforce Service Pilots (WASP).[35] A woman named Anne Mohammed, for instance, signed up for the Cadet Nursing Corps at University of Michigan—Ann Arbor, though for some reason did not complete her training.[36]

These were not the only Muslims to serve in World War II; the places of birth listed on Muslim draft registration cards include locations such as Afghanistan, Java, India, Malaya, Persia, Singapore, and Sumatra—countries whose dominant ethnic group are not Arabic-speaking people. For example, a man named Shrieff Mohammed enlisted in 1943. A resident of New York, he was listed as coming from Balochistan or another part of the British East Indies.[37]

World War II marked the beginning of a turning point in the history of Muslim members of the US military. In the second half of the twentieth century, Muslim representation in the military came to reflect the ethnic and racial diversity of Muslim Americans themselves. The story of Muslim soldiers, sailors, airmen, and marines in the second half of the twentieth century became a story of white, black, and brown Americans whose collective cultural heritage was echoed in the armed forces of the United States. They performed acts of heroism in combat but they also served in peacetime and in noncombat roles.

In the second half of the twentieth century, Muslim Americans became important to military history in another way. Some African American Muslims became symbols of protest against mandatory military service and against US wars in the developing world. The story of Muslim Americans in the military would be incomplete without including some consideration of those Muslims who refused, on principle, to serve.

Notes

1. Clinton Bennett, "United States Military," in *Encyclopedia of Muslim-American History*, ed. Edward E. Curtis IV (New York: Facts on File, 2010), 561.

2. Allan D. Austin, *African Muslims in Antebellum America: Transatlantic Stories and Spiritual Struggles* (New York: Routledge, 1997).

3. Mary V. Thompson, "Mounty Vernon," in *Encyclopedia of Muslim-American History*, ed. Edward E. Curtis IV (New York: Facts on File, 2010), 391–394.

4. Austin, *African Muslims in Antebellum America*, 265, 268.

5. My account of the Camel Corps above comes mainly from Charles C. Carroll, "The Government's Importation of Camels: A Historical Sketch," in *Twentieth Annual Report of the Bureau of Animal Industry* (Washington, DC: U.S. Department of Agriculture, Government Printing Office, 1904), 391–409.

6. *U. S., Returns from Military Posts, 1806–1916* (Provo, UT: Ancestry.com, 2009).

7. Jay J. Wagoner, *Early Arizona: Prehistory to Civil War* (Tucson: University of Arizona Press, 1975), 339–344.

8. "Hi Jolly's Tomb," Trip Advisor, accessed September 2, 2016, https://www.tripadvisor.com/Attraction_Review-g31325-d7140143-Reviews-Hi_Jolly_s_Tomb-Quartzsite_Arizona.html.

9. The legacy of Hadji Ali is covered in Steve Frangos, "Philip Tedro: A Greek Legend of the American West," updated November 26, 2007, http://www.helleniccomserve.com/philiptedro.html.

10. *Compiled Military Service Records of Volunteer Union Soldiers Who Served with the United States Colored Troops: 1st through 5th United States Colored Cavalry, 5th Massachusetts Cavalry (Colored), 6th United States Colored Cavalry* as reproduced in *U.S., Colored Troops Military Service Records, 1863–1865* (Provo, UT: Ancestry.com, 2007).

11. Unless otherwise noted, all quotations from Said and my account of his life come Nicholas Said, *The Autobiography of Nicholas Said; a Native of Bornou, Eastern Soudan, Central Africa* (Memphis, TN: Shotwell and Company, 1873), 9–224, http://docsouth.unc.edu/neh/said/said.html.

12. "Teaching with Documents: The Fight for Equal Rights: Black Soldiers in the Civil War," National Archives, accessed September 2, 2016, https://www.archives.gov/education/lessons/blacks-civil-war/.

13. Historical Data Systems, comp. *U.S., Civil War Soldier Records and Profiles, 1861–1865* (Provo, UT: Ancestry.com, 2009).

14. Their stories are detailed, among other places, in Edward E. Curtis IV, ed., *Encyclopedia of Muslim-American History* (New York: Facts on File, 2010).

15. Amir Muhammad, *Muslim Veterans of American Wars: Revolutionary War, War of 1812, Civil War, World War I & II* (Washington, DC: FreeMan Publications, 2007).

16. *Compiled Military Service Records of Volunteer Union Soldiers Who Served with the United States Colored Troops: Artillery Organizations* as reproduced in *U.S., Colored Troops Military Service Records, 1863–1865* (Provo, UT: Ancestry.com, 2007); *Annual Report of the Adjutant General* as reproduced in *U.S., Adjutant General Military Records, 1631–1976* (Provo, UT: Ancestry.com, 2011).

17. Jonathan Deiss, "Ali ben Moussa, a real Zouave," *Vulnus Sclopeticum* (blog), August 11, 2011, http://soldiersource.blogspot.com/2011/08/ali-ben-moussa-real -zouave.html.

18. *Compiled Military Service Records of Volunteer Union Soldiers Who Served with the United States Colored Troops: 1st through 5th United States Colored Cavalry, 5th Massachusetts Cavalry (Colored), 6th United States Colored Cavalry*; Microfilm Serial: M1801; Microfilm Roll: 16 as reproduced in *U.S., Colored Troops Military Service Records, 1863–1865* (Provo, UT, USA: Ancestry.com, 2007).

19. Richard M. Reid, ed., *Practicing Medicine in a Black Regiment: The Civil War Diary of Burt G. Wilder* (Amherst, MA: University of Massachusetts Press, 2010), 239–240.

20. *Compiled Military Service Records of Volunteer Union Soldiers Who Served with the United States Colored Troops: 1st through 5th United States Colored Cavalry, 5th Massachusetts Cavalry (Colored), 6th United States Colored Cavalry* as reproduced in *U.S., Colored Troops Military Service Records, 1863–1865* (Provo, UT: Ancestry.com, 2007).

21. My account of Omer Otmen and Company K is based on Victor F. Barnett, *A History of the Activities and Operations of the 360th United States Infantry Regiment in the World War, 1914–1918* (Zeltigen, Germany: American Expeditionary Forces, 1919), http://www.90thdivisionassoc.org/90thdivisionfolders/mervinbooks /WWI360/WWI36001.pdf.

22. "United States World War I Draft Registration Cards, 1917–1918," Washington, DC: National Archives and Records Administration, n.d.; FHL microfilm 1,711,447.

23. *Roster of the Men and Women who served in the Army or Naval Service (including the Marine Corps) of the United States or its Allies from the State of North Dakota in the World War, 1917–1918, Volume 3*, as reproduced in *North Dakota Military Men, 1917–1918* (Provo, UT: Ancestry.com, 2000).

24. Philip K. Hitti, *Syrians in America* (New York: George H. Doran, 1924), 102.

25. For an introduction to Arab American history, see Gregory Orfalea, *The Arab Americans: A History* (Northhampton, MA: Olive Branch Press, 2006).

26. The surname "Mondul," for example, was shared by nineteen registered persons whose race was listed as Indian (Oriental), Indian (Red), Malay, and white. Their first names include Shaikh Abdur Rahman, Abdul Jobber, Abdul Hamed, and Abdul Wahed.

27. The best account of North Dakota's Syrian community is William C. Sherman, Paul L. Whitney, and John Guerrero, *Prairie Peddlers: The Syrian-Lebanese in North Dakota* (Bismarck, ND: University of Mary Press, 2002).

28. *Applications for Headstones for U.S. Military Veterans, 1925–1941*, Records of the Office of the Quartermaster General, Record Group 92, National Archives at Washington, DC, as reproduced in *U.S., Headstone Applications for Military Veterans, 1925–1963* (Provo, UT: Ancestry.com, 2012). See also Gregory Orfalea, "Mosque on the Prairie," in ed. Eric Hoglund, vol. 2, *Taking Root* (Washington, DC: Arab American Anti-Discrimination Committee, 1985), 11, http://files.eric.ed.gov/fulltext /ED361275.pdf.

29. Applications for Headstones for US Military Veterans, 1925–1941. Microfilm publication M1916. ARC ID: 596118. Records of the Office of the Quartermaster General, Record Group 92. National Archives and Records Administration at Washington, DC.

30. Patrick Callaway, "North Dakota," in *Encyclopedia of Muslim-American History*, ed. Edward E. Curtis IV (New York: Facts on File, 2010), 438–439.

31. See further Sherman, Whitney, and Guerrero, *Prairie Peddlers*, for the whole story.

32. Kassam Rameden, North Dakota Writers' Project Ethnic Group Files c. 1935–1942, Microfilm Roll 3, State Historical Society of North Dakota. All quotations from Rameden are from this interview. Rameden's life is known to us not only through the fragmentary evidence provided by census, military, and immigration records but also because in 1939, he gave a full interview to William A. Glen, who was employed by the government-funded agency Works Progress Administration (WPA). A product of President Franklin D. Roosevelt's New Deal for the American people, the WPA funded numerous employment programs across the country, including artists, dramatic performances, writers, and a program devoted to recording the rich ethnic heritage of the United States.

33. John Omar's recollections of his service are collected in "Arab Americans and the U.S. Military" a website part of a 2003 course taught at Michigan State University by Dr. Rosina Hassoun. See "John R. Omar," Michigan State University, updated April 24, 2003, https://msu.edu/course/iah/211c/hassoun/content/arabsmilitary /Soldier9.htm.

34. "John R. Omar," *Patriot Ledger*, May 19, 2007, http://www.legacy.com /obituaries/southofboston-ledger/obituary.aspx?n=john-r-omar&pid=88164094; "World War II," in *Encyclopedia of Muslim-American History*, ed. Edward E. Curtis IV (New York: Facts on File, 2010), 593.

35. Shareda Hosein, "Military: Women's Participation: United States," in *Encyclopedia of Women and Islamic Cultures*, vol. 2, ed. Suad Joseph (2005), http:// sjoseph.ucdavis.edu/ewic-public-outreach-resources/ewic-outreach-resources /military-womens-participation-united-states.

36. National Archives and Records Administration, Washington, DC; *Cadet Nurse Corps Files, compiled 1943–1948, documenting the period 1942–1948*; Box #223 as reproduced in *U.S., World War II Cadet Nursing Corps Card Files, 1942–1948* (Provo, UT: Ancestry.com, 2011).

37. "Access to Archival Databases," National Archives, accessed September 2, 2016, https://aad.archives.gov/aad/record-detail.jsp?dt=893&mtch=1&cat =GP23&tf=F&q=shrieff+mohammed&bc=sl&rpp=10&pg=1&rid=3299949.

THREE

PATRIOTISM AND PROTEST: FROM WORLD WAR II TO THE GULF WAR

IN THE SECOND HALF OF THE TWENTIETH CENTURY, Muslim Americans continued their commitment to military service. They served in the Korean War (1950–1953), the Vietnam War (1955–1975), and the Gulf War (1990–1991).

In the 1950s, some of them decided it was time for the military to recognize them as Muslims. Coming home from World War II, Muslim service members thought it was wrong that, unlike Christians and Jews, they were not allowed to be identified as Muslims on their dog tags, the identification tags generally worn around a service member's neck.

World War II veteran Abdullah Igram (1923–1981) of Cedar Rapids, Iowa, decided to do something about it. Igram had served in the Philippines during World War II. In 1954, he helped establish the Federation of Islamic Associations of the United States and Canada (FIA). The FIA went on to be largest ecumenical national Muslim organization in the 1950s. It was an umbrella group for Sunni and Shia religious congregations as well as youth associations and ethnic clubs. Though dominated by Arab Americans, its membership included Pakistani, Albanian, Iranian, and African Americans.[1]

The year before he convened the first official meeting of the FIA, Igram had written to President Dwight D. Eisenhower, who had been the supreme commander of Allied forces in World War II. Catholics, Jews, and Protestants were allowed to have their religious identity marked on the dog tags, and Igram asked that Muslims be afforded that privilege too.

This was extremely important not only to recognize the contributions of Muslims but also for proper protocol in case the soldier, sailor, airman, or marine died while serving. Without indicating that the service member belonged to the Islamic faith (marked with an "I" for Islam), he or she would not receive a proper Islamic burial. "Everybody got their dog tags, and mine had an 'X' for no religion," remembered Pvt. Ace Aossey. "I came back from boot camp and Abdullah Igram said, 'No, you've got to have that changed.' And I did." President Eisenhower's administration first balked at the request. But the Department of Defense eventually came to agree and decided that Muslims must be able to add their religious identity on their ID tags.[2]

Muslim American contributions to the United States in the second half of the twentieth century went beyond loyal service to the military. Perhaps the greatest contribution that Muslim Americans made to the nation during this historical period was their principled opposition to US wars in the developing world, especially in the Southeast Asian country of Vietnam. The refusal of one man in particular, world boxing champion Muhammad Ali, to serve during the Vietnam War—and even more, his willingness to give up his boxing title and go to jail rather than flee the country—stands as one of the greatest profiles in courage in US history.

AFRICAN AMERICAN MUSLIM OPPOSITION TO WAR

Thousands of Muslims served in the military from World War II to the Vietnam War. And Muhammad Ali was one of hundreds of Muslims who, on principle, refused to do so.

The Muslims who would not serve were, by and large, African Americans who were denied equal rights by the US government into the 1960s. A century after the legal end of slavery, African Americans still lived in a federally sanctioned system of white supremacy called Jim Crow. Outside of the South, though black people were, in theory, entitled to equal rights, they were the victims of harsh racial discrimination wherever they went. They were systematically discriminated against in education and denied equal access to decent housing. They were the victims of unfair policing and prosecution. Perhaps worst of all, their bodies could be beaten, experimented on, and even sterilized without their consent.[3]

After World War II, one African American Muslim group, known as the Nation of Islam, rose to national attention for its fight against American racism. A man named W. D. Fard Muhammad founded the organization in Detroit, Michigan, in 1930. After World War II ended in 1945, his follower, Elijah Muhammad (1897–1975), rose to national attention as its leader. The Honorable Elijah Muhammad, as his followers called him, was one of millions of African Americans who came north in the Great Migration from rural areas of the South. He taught a novel form of Islamic religion. Contradicting the basic tenets of both Sunni and Shia Islam, he proclaimed that Fard Muhammad was God in the flesh and he, rather than Prophet Muhammad of Arabia (d. 632 CE), was the Messenger of God. No other Muslim group around the world would accept such an assertion, but that did not prevent some of these international Muslims from attempting to engage in what became the most prominent Islamic movement in the United States after World War II.[4]

The group was called the *Nation* of Islam for a reason. According to its teachings, black Americans, denied their God-given human rights by the white government, were foreigners inside of the United States. They were part of a different nation, a global nation that was composed of all people of color around the globe. Their original religion was Islam, the Messenger taught. The bodies and the minds of blacks/Muslims had been enslaved for centuries, according to the movement's teachings, but now a prophet had come to mentally resurrect them from the graveyard, which was said to be the United States and Christianity. They should separate from their former slave masters, said their leader. Elijah Muhammad opposed racial integration. Instead he encouraged the development of separate black neighborhoods, businesses, schools, and other cultural institutions. He told his followers that they should not serve in the US military, and he was willing to put his own body on the line for these religious beliefs. In World War II, Muhammad and dozens of other Nation of Islam members were convicted of draft evasion and went to prison.

His son and eventual heir, Wallace Delaney Muhammad (1933–2008), later known as Imam W. D. Mohammed, was willing to do the same. In 1953, during the end of the United States' war in Korea, Muhammad became eligible for the military draft. He asked his local draft board in Chicago to classify him as a conscientious objector (CO) on the grounds that his religion prohibited him from participating in the military. Muhammad was granted CO status, and in 1957, was told that he could serve two years at the Illinois State Hospital instead of regular military duty. But he refused and did not report for duty. In 1958, the federal government brought charges against him, and he was convicted of draft evasion. His father's legal team appealed, but the three-year-long conviction was upheld. In 1961, Muhammad reported to the Sandstone Federal Correctional

Institution in Minnesota to serve his time. He was paroled on January 10, 1963.[5]

As mentioned, the most consequential example of a Nation of Islam believer willing to go to prison for refusal to serve in the US military was that of Muhammad Ali (1942–2016). Born Cassius Marcellus Clay Jr. in Louisville, Kentucky, he began boxing at the age of twelve. While still a teenager, Clay won two national Golden Gloves titles and a gold medal in light heavyweight boxing at the Rome Olympics in 1960. Soon after, he began to hear about the Nation of Islam and attended religious services in Miami after he turned from amateur to professional boxing.[6]

On February 24, 1964, Clay stunned the boxing world when he defeated heavyweight champion Sonny Liston. Clay's religious adviser, Malcolm X (1925–1965), was on hand to see the victory. Soon afterward, Clay made public his identity as a Muslim. *Sports Illustrated* declared that Clay was "a member of the Black Muslim cult, a twisted form of Islam that advocates racial separatism." This is not how Clay himself put it. He believed in "Allah and in peace," he said. "Islam is a religion and there are 750 million people all over the world who believe in it, and I am one of them."[7] Elijah Muhammad then granted Clay an Islamic name, Muhammad Ali. Some members of the public became hysterical. He received death threats.

Then, in 1967, the world heavyweight boxing champion refused to be inducted into the US Army. Ali's courage to stand up for his beliefs was as remarkable as his fearlessness in the boxing ring. He attended his army induction ceremony at the Military Entrance Processing Station in Houston, Texas. His name was called. He refused to step forward. Ali was warned that he could spend up to five years in prison. Still, he refused. Eventually he was arrested and convicted of draft evasion.

By 1967, the US involvement in the Vietnam War, a civil war that pitted North Vietnam against South Vietnam, had become unpopular among many US citizens. US involvement in the country that the occupying French referred to as Indochina began as early as 1950 and increased after 1954, when French colonial forces were defeated in the Battle of Dien Bien Phu. But the United States did not declare all-out war against the North Vietnamese until 1964, when the Gulf of Tonkin Resolution authorized President Lyndon Johnson to conduct whatever military operations he deemed necessary. By 1967, almost half a million armed service members were committed to the conflict. Thousands of them were killed, and large numbers of Americans came to oppose US involvement in Vietnam.[8]

Lt. Col. J. Edwin McKee leads Muhammad Ali away from the induction ceremony in which the boxing champion refused to join the US armed forces. (Associated Press.)[9]

Ali said he was a CO who could not serve in the military because his faith prohibited killing. The year before, when his draft status had been altered to make him eligible for the draft, Ali had given a much lengthier explanation of his refusal to fight:

> Why should they ask me to put on a uniform and go ten thousand miles from home and drop bombs and bullets on brown people in Vietnam while so-called Negro people in Louisville are treated like dogs and denied simple human rights?
>
> No, I am not going ten thousand miles from home to help murder and burn another poor nation simply to continue the domination of white slave masters of the darker people the world over. This is the day when such evils must come to an end. I have been warned that to take such a stand would put my prestige in jeopardy and could cause me to lose millions of dollars which should accrue to me as the champion.
>
> But I have said it once and I will say it again. The real enemy of my people is right here. I will not disgrace my religion, my people or

myself by becoming a tool to enslave those who are fighting for their own justice, freedom and equality . . .

If I thought the war was going to bring freedom and equality to 22 million of my people they wouldn't have to draft me, I'd join tomorrow. But I either have to obey the laws of the land or the laws of Allah. I have nothing to lose by standing up for my beliefs. So I'll go to jail. We've been in jail for four hundred years.[10]

This principled stance cost him dearly. Ali was stripped of his heavyweight boxing title, his state boxing licenses were taken away, and he wasn't allowed to leave the country.

But in 1971, Ali's conviction was overturned by the US Supreme Court. He had stood up to the government of the most powerful nation on earth, and he had scored a moral victory. That year, he fought heavyweight champ Joe Frazier. Ali lost. But in a 1974 bout called the "Rumble in the Jungle" in Kinshasa, Zaire, with the new heavyweight champ, George Foreman, Ali emerged victorious. Once again, Ali's boxing prowess stunned the world. The heavily favored Foreman, known for his hard punching, was defeated not so much by Ali's quick moves but by a rope-a-dope strategy in which Ali absorbed Foreman's blows round after round and then pounced after Foreman became tired.

President Gerald R. Ford invited Ali, the man who had refused to be inducted into the US Army, to the White House. It was a sign of changing times, as many Americans sought to heal the stark divisions that US involvement in the Vietnam War had created in the country. The visit also signaled a rapprochement between members of the Nation of Islam and the US military.

AFRICAN AMERICAN MUSLIM MILITARY SERVICE AFTER 1975

It is one of the great ironies of US military history that Nation of Islam leader Imam W. D. Mohammed, a man who had served a sentence in federal prison for refusing even non-combatant service to the military in the 1950s, became one of the US military's most important Muslim American supporters in the last quarter of the twentieth century. Explaining how this occurred means looking first at leadership changes in the Nation of Islam after 1975.

In 1975, Mohammed assumed the leadership of the Nation of Islam from his father, Elijah Muhammad. Over the next several years, the son would transform the father's legacy. He abandoned the claim that W. D. Fard Muhammad was God and that his father was a prophet. Mohammed, who became known as Imam, or Leader, said instead that God, known in Arabic as Allah, had never taken human form. Prophet Muhammad of Arabia (d. 632) was the last Messenger of God, not his father, said the Imam. Mohammed asked his followers to pray five times a day, fast during the Islamic month of Ramadan, and go on hajj, or pilgrimage to Mecca. In other words, Mohammed turned the Nation of Islam toward the basic religious beliefs and practices of most Sunni and Shia Muslims.

In addition to adopting these Islamic religious traditions, Mohammed encouraged his followers to become American patriots. The Nation of Islam had preached that African Americans were not really American, but one year after taking over the leadership of the movement, Mohammed proudly displayed the US flag at official events. In 1977, he announced that his followers, whom he said were striving to be "model American citizens," should celebrate "New World Patriotism Day." The US flag appeared on *Bilalian News*, the movement's newspaper. Children in its parochial schools recited the Pledge of Allegiance. By 1979, one of the businesses associated with the movement signed a $22 million contract to supply the US Department of Defense with food packs.[11]

Not all of his followers liked these changes. The single most prominent among them was Minister Louis Farrakhan, who by 1978 had left the group to restart a version of the original of Nation of Islam.

However, a large group of followers not only stayed in the movement—they took Mohammed's patriotism to heart. As long as the United States supported Muslims' freedom to practice their religion, he preached in the 1980s, Muslims had an obligation to support their country. Military service was no longer compulsory for males in the United States—the draft ended in 1973—but Mohammed encouraged believers to serve in the military.

S.Sgt. Lyndon Bilal, the current commander of the Muslim American Veterans Association, exemplified Mohammed's ethic of patriotic responsibility. Raised in Gary, Indiana, Bilal came to know about Islamic religion from his older brother, who converted while Bilal was still in high school. At first, Bilal made fun of his brother for giving up drinking and smoking and eating pork. But eventually he came to admire his dignity, strength, and religious knowledge.[12]

In 1980, Bilal joined the air force. He failed an inspection when a technical instructor discovered copies of *Bilalian News* in his drawer. Then Airman Bilal was brought before his sergeant, who dramatically asked, "Who is your leader?"

"Wallace D. Mohammed," Bilal answered.

And the sergeant said, "He's my leader, too."

After basic training, Bilal completed eight months of electronics training at Naval Station Great Lakes in Illinois and then six months of specialized technical training at Chanute Air Force Base, also in Illinois.

In 1981, Bilal took his *shahada*, or profession of faith, while he was posted at Wright-Patterson Air Force Base in Ohio. He formally stood before other believers at a mosque in Springfield, Ohio, and recited, "I witness that there is no god but God; I witness that Muhammad is the Messenger of God."

At the time, there were no official Muslim chaplains in the military and few instances of Islamic religious services and celebrations. Wherever Bilal was stationed, he sought to become a lay leader and to establish regular Friday congregational prayers. Becoming a lay leader meant obtaining a letter from a local religious institution that he was qualified to lead the Friday prayers. Bilal also worked closely with existing chaplains, whose job it was to serve the religious needs of all service members, no matter their religious affiliation.

After a two-year post in Ankara, Turkey, Bilal took a job at the Pentagon, where he established regular Friday prayers for employees and military personnel at the country's defense headquarters. Inspired by Imam W. D. Mohammed, Bilal began to advocate for the appointment of Muslim chaplains in the US military as part of a group called Muslim Military Members. If Jews, Protestants, and Catholics could have their own chaplains, then Muslims should too, they asserted.

In 1990 and 1991, Mohammed became a strong supporter of Operations Desert Shield and Desert Storm, which would come to be known as the Gulf War. In August 1990, Iraqi leader Saddam Hussein invaded Kuwait after failed negotiations concerning the theft of Iraqi oil and a Kuwaiti-Iraqi border dispute. US President George H. W. Bush, a strong ally of Kuwait and other oil-producing countries in the Persian Gulf, assembled an international coalition of dozens of countries, including some Muslim countries, to expel Saddam Hussein's Iraqi military from Kuwait. Mohammed traveled to Saudi Arabia, the main staging area for the coalition, to support the Saudi alliance with the United States.

On February 5, 1992, the Pentagon held a lunch in Mohammed's honor, with Bilal serving as host. It was held the day before he became the first Muslim to open a session of the US Senate with an invocation. Even Muhammad Ali attended the luncheon. In introducing Moham-

Imam W. D. Mohammed, son and heir of Elijah Muhammad, receives an award from Sgt. Lyndon Bilal at the Pentagon in 1992. (Photo courtesy of Commander Lyndon Bilal.)

med, Department of Defense chaplain Stanley Esterline lauded his "great contribution to our nation, bringing people of all faiths into harmony and understanding." He thanked him for his "loyal and unswerving religious leadership in support of our nation during the difficult times of the Gulf War," and called him a "great American, a great Muslim leader." Toward the end of the speech, Mohammed put his hand on Bilal's shoulder, saying, "I would like to be in uniform and I'd like to be an officer, just like this officer." "This was the highlight of my military career," said Bilal in an interview.[13]

Mohammed's support of the military and the influence of his followers inside the Pentagon helped pave the way in 1993 for the first US Army Muslim chaplain, Lt. Col. Abdul-Rasheed Muhammad. Over his military career of almost twenty years, Muhammad served as a chaplain with the Twenty-Eighth Combat Support Hospital at Fort Bragg, North Carolina; the Second Battalion, Ninth Infantry Regiment at Camp Casey, Korea; Walter Reed Army Medical Center, Washington, DC; the Fourth Brigade, First Calvary Division, in Fort Hood, Texas; the First Infantry Division, in Kitzingen, Germany; and the US Army Chaplain Center and School in Fort Jackson, South Carolina.

It is important to keep in mind that not all African American Muslims who joined the armed forces in this era were former members of the Nation of Islam motivated by a newfound sense of patriotism. African Americans who practiced a Sunni form of Islam were not as well-known as followers of the Nation of Islam, but some of them served before 1975.

Perhaps more importantly, it is vital to remember that many poor and working-class Americans—of various religious and racial backgrounds— have sometimes served in America's all-volunteer armed forces after 1973 because they thought the military was their best hope for an education, employment, and even room and board.

Imam Zaid Shakir, who was the main officiant at the 2016 funeral prayers for boxer Muhammad Ali, was one of them. After dropping out of college, Shakir joined the air force because he "needed a roof over my head and food in my stomach, and I wanted to continue my education." In his memoirs, Shakir remembers that the situation was "depressing" since, at that time, he "viewed the armed forces as epitomizing American imperialism." But Shakir figured that the Vietnam War "was over, and that I would not be called on to participate killing anyone in the name of 'God and country.'"[14]

Shakir went to basic training at Lackland Air Force Base in San Antonio, Texas, and then technical training in Denver, Colorado. He was posted to Barksdale Air Force Base in Louisiana. There, in 1977, after a lot of meditating, reading, and studying, he decided to convert to Islam. When Shakir was sent to serve at Incirlik Air Base in Turkey, a member of the NATO Alliance, he helped form an Islamic study group. The Turkish base commander demanded that they stop, saying that their religious activities violated the secular laws of the country. Even then, some other members of the armed forces who studied with Shakir and other Muslims converted to Islam. From his service in the military, Shakir would go on to be a highly skilled scholar of Sharia, cofounder of a Muslim liberal arts college, and one of the most prominent Muslim religious leaders in the United States.

MUSLIM IMMIGRANTS AND THE MILITARY SERVICE OF THEIR DAUGHTERS

In 1965, President Lyndon Johnson signed an immigration reform bill that did away with the racially discriminatory quotas enshrined in the Immigration Act of 1924. Under the old system, the annual quotas for immigrants were set at 149,667 Europeans, 2,990 Asians, and 1,400 Africans. The new Immigration and Nationality Act of 1965, also known as the Hart-Celler Act, which took effect in 1968, no longer favored immigrants from northwestern Europe. Instead, it gave preference to the relatives of US citizens and permanent residents and to professionals such as engineers, scientists, and physicians. The total number of visas issued would be limited, but not because you came from Africa, Asia, or Latin America. This new law transformed the United States, most notably through large-scale immigration from Latin America.

It also changed the face of Muslim America. Perhaps a million or more Muslims arrived in the United States by the end of the twentieth century. Though the US government does not keep track of the religions of its immigrants, it is safe to conclude that hundreds of thousands of the immigrants who arrived from the Middle East and South Asia were Muslim. They would be joined later by perhaps hundreds of thousands of Muslims from sub-Saharan Africa.

Up to this point in Muslim American history, it is possible that the Nation of Islam, the group led by Elijah Muhammad, had as many or perhaps more mosques than any other single Muslim organization. The Nation of Islam also had what was probably the largest single Muslim parochial school system, called the University of Islam and later renamed the Clara Muhammad Schools. In the decades after 1965, all of that changed. Immigrants established approximately a thousand new mosques and hundreds of Islamic elementary or secondary schools. They created national organizations such as the Islamic Society of North America and the Islamic Circle of North America, among others. They opened businesses, media outlets, professional organizations, and other institutions that catered to a growing Muslim American community.

Like most immigrants, these Muslim Americans hoped to live the American dream. They worked hard. Some of them were professionals and achieved noteworthy success. Fazlur Rahman Khan engineered the Sears (now Willis) Tower and the John Hancock Center in Chicago. Ahmed Zewail of the California Institute of Technology received the Nobel Prize in Chemistry. Many working-class immigrants worked long hours in service industries, hoping their children would get an education and achieve financial success. For those who were religiously observant, America was seen as a place, often very different from their home countries, where they were free to practice Islam in the way they thought best. In various opinion polls, these Muslim immigrants reported that they were happy in America—happier than the average American because they were grateful for their new lives.[15]

Called by a sense of patriotic duty, their sons and daughters sometimes decided to join the US military. Some of these daughters even joined against the wishes of their fathers. "My father was strongly against me joining the navy," former PO First Class Fatima Ahmed remembered.[16] "My father had chosen an all-girls college for me and was going to cover all college and housing expenses but I preferred to be self-sufficient and longed for independence." When a marine recruiter came to her school in greater Chicago, she decided to speak with him on a dare. But then Ahmed's stepmother encouraged her to take it seriously. "I had also recently watched the movie GI Jane," said Ahmed, "and was inspired by the portrayal of a strong and fearless woman in the military. I wanted to see what I was capable of mentally and physically. I knew there was a chance it could break me, but I felt like it was something I had to do."

It was a long way from the remote Egyptian village that Ahmed had left when she immigrated to the United States as a seven-year-old. Serving in the US Navy on active duty from 1998 to 2006 and then in the reserves from 2007 to 2009, Ahmed encountered numerous challenges, only some of which were on account of her Muslim heritage. "The rampant sexual harassment nearly destroyed me," she said. "I grew up in a very sheltered life and did not know how to cope with men, some considerably older than me. They made lewd comments and propositions, and there were consequences for rejecting them." The swim test that she had to take was particularly hard because Ahmed had never worn a swimsuit in front of men. "I often felt conflicted, uncomfortable, and out of place," she said about her life in the navy. "I was surrounded by people consuming alcohol, and even when I was underage, I had people trying to get me to drink and I refused. I witnessed many things I would prefer I had not—like people going to strip clubs or having casual relationships. It made me question whether I was too uptight or something was wrong with me. But I also drew strength from my faith, which helped stabilize my world, which seemed at times out of control."

There were also aspects of life in the navy that Ahmed loved, especially the strength of the friendships that she formed and the sense of family that she cultivated. "Despite some negative experiences," she stated, "I consider joining the navy one of the best decisions of my life. The navy played a major role in helping me become a stronger person, learn who I am and what I believe, and afforded me many advantages personally and professionally. My time in the navy is a major part of my identity."

Though he was initially opposed to her entering the navy, her father eventually came around. When she was awarded Direct Report Sailor of the Year, he proudly attended the ceremony at the Pentagon. Her stepmother, who wears a head scarf, was also in attendance. She was worried that she might receive some negative comments or looks, but nothing happened. The event made Ahmed "reflect on my journey from being an outsider who was not at all accepted as an American to where I was at that moment"—in the country's defense headquarters, her father and stepmother watching as she was honored by her adopted country. Even the backlash on Muslims due to the attacks of 9/11 were not as bad as she initially feared. "When I arrived at work that day," she remembered, "I was called into the office of my Commanding Officer (CO) and Executive Officer (XO). I did not know what to expect. I was relieved to hear them tell me that they fully supported me and to come to them if I had any issues or if there was any backlash. I had some ignorant comments and questions from others in the command, but overall nothing too negative."

Ahmed completed a BS in information systems with a focus on homeland security. Her work in the navy revolved around information technologies, and she served as a local area network (LAN) administrator, information assurance manager, and space systems operator (dealing with satellites). After leaving the navy, she took jobs with BAE Systems, which worked with the Federal Bureau of Investigation (FBI), and she did a project for the Hashemite Kingdom of Jordan while employed at Hewlett Packard Enterprise Services. She now works at the Federal Energy Regulatory Commission. She is also married. But Ahmed can't quite let go of the navy. In fact, she is thinking about joining the navy reserves.

Perhaps Ahmed's story is not so unusual among the children who came with their immigrant parents after 1965. Lt. Col. Shareda Hosein, for instance, is another immigrant's daughter who decided to join the US military without getting her parents' approval. Hosein arrived in the United States in 1972 with her parents, Abidh and Ojeefan Hosein, and four younger brothers and sisters. They were Muslims of Indian descent from the Caribbean nation of Trinidad and Tobago. They settled in Dorchester, Massachusetts, where her father worked as a cable splicer for the telephone company and the family frequently socialized with other Trinidadians. Her parents were strict, but Hosein just wanted to blend in. She wasn't allowed to go out on dates or stay out late. She played sports after school and then came home. The family attended the Islamic Center of New England, but the lessons that she received in Islamic Sunday school did not always speak to her as a teenager wanting to live what she saw as a normal teenage life.[17]

The summer between Hosein's junior and senior year at Boston Latin Academy, a high school known for high academic achievement, she visited Germany. It gave her the travel bug, and she wanted to return to Germany after she graduated. During her senior year, Hosein was unsure where she would go to college or what she would do after graduation. That's when she discovered the US armed services. Reading a magazine, Hosein saw an advertisement for some free socks from the US Army. She sent the card in for the socks, and the next thing she knew, she was being recruited. Recruiters told her that she would earn money for college and get to go to Germany again. It was the promise of returning to Germany that did the trick.

In 1979, during her senior year, Hosein turned eighteen, and without consulting with her parents, she signed the recruitment contract. When she told her father, his immediate response was, "Could you kill someone?" Hosein admitted to herself that she had not thought this all the way through. She didn't talk about that with the recruiter. From what she understood, she would be working a desk, not a gun. In retrospect, she wished that she had consulted with her parents more. But at the time, she was excited to be an adult, ready to make her own decisions. She was tired of the strict rules at home. She was declaring her independence. Hosein was a big fan of John Wayne and movies such as *The Guns of Navarone*, and even though she didn't want to fight, she certainly could embrace the American value of rugged individualism.[18]

Pvt. Hosein attended basic training at Fort Jackson, South Carolina, and was posted as a clerk typist to Headquarters Company, Second Armored Division in West Germany. She was then sent to Panama but requested an early discharge because she was expecting a baby. Hosein enrolled at the University of Massachusetts in Boston, but she missed the military life and decided to join the reserves. In 1986, she attended Officer Candidate School at Fort Benning, Georgia, and the next year, she graduated with her bachelor's degree in business and marketing. Second Lt. Hosein then started selling real estate.

In 1987, Hosein became a personnel officer and, after that, a transportation officer focused on logistics. For years, her unit would train to load large transport ships in case of war. They would travel to ports in Georgia,

Lt. Col. Shareda Hosein served in the US Army and army reserves for more than thirty-five years. (Photo by Bob Croslin.)

North Carolina, and Texas to manage the loading of trucks, jeeps, helicopter, and tanks that needed to be sent overseas. During the Gulf War in 1990–1991, her unit was deployed to offload the transport ships that were returning from the conflict. Hosein eventually left logistics and returned to personnel work, serving as the commander of a postal unit. Then, in 2004, she was mobilized for ten months during the Iraq War. Her unit in

Kuwait was responsible for making sure the mail was delivered, keeping track of the whereabouts of all service members involved in the conflict, and reporting on service members who were injured or killed. The job was intense. She would work twelve to eighteen hours a day, sometimes seven days a week.

In 2007, Hosein became a cultural engagement officer at the US Special Operations Command (SOCOM). Her mission was to educate her colleagues about Islam and Muslims. Since both wars in Iraq and Afghanistan were in the Muslim-majority countries, it was important to her to explain the diversity of Muslims, especially the difference between al-Qaeda's understanding of Islam and that of almost every other Muslim. Hosein would answer questions about the Qur'an and bring in outside speakers to deliver guest lectures at SOCOM.[19]

Hosein was also working toward a different job in the military during this time. She wanted to become the first female Muslim chaplain in the military. In 2001, this idea became a calling. She was posted in Kuwait and was hanging out in the base chapel. Another female soldier who had converted to Islam was having trouble performing ablutions—the ritual cleansing, generally with water, of the hands, mouth, face, forearms, head, ears, and feet—that one is supposed to do before making daily prayers. A male Muslim chaplain asked Hosein to help out. The two women went to the bathroom, and Hosein demonstrated how to do the ritual washing. This was the sign that confirmed her heart's desire to become a chaplain. "I got so choked up," she said in one interview, "because I had prayed to God, asking, 'Is this the right thing for me to do?' And I was like: 'You can't get a bigger sign than this. You just can't.' And so I helped her. The man led the prayer. And we prayed."[20]

Hosein was already enrolled in Hartford Seminary's Islamic chaplaincy program, which would grant her the master's degree in divinity generally recognized as a necessary qualification for any chaplaincy, whether in the military or civilian life. In 2003, she submitted her application to the military to become a full-time chaplain. In 2004, while in Kuwait, she met the chief of staff for the army's chief of chaplains. As Hosein later recalled, "He pretty much said, 'Hey, we'd love to have you. We need you, but you can't lead prayers with men and women. So, you can't come on board.'" The official was referring to the fact that almost all Muslims understand Sharia, or Islamic law and ethics, as requiring males to lead the prayers when men and women are both in attendance. The army had decided that because Hosein could not perform all of the ritual functions of a male chaplain, she could not become a chaplain in any capacity. The military maintained the same policy for women who wanted to become Roman Catholic chaplains. Because the Roman Catholic Church reserves certain rituals only for male priests, the military figured that it too would hire only male Roman Catholic chaplains.

Hosein said that the military simply misunderstood the role of the imam in Islamic religion. Lt. Col. Abdul-Rasheed Muhammad, the military's first Muslim chaplain, supported her application and hoped that the army would change its mind. "She doesn't have to lead men in prayer to be chaplain. That's the bottom line," he explained. Unlike Roman Catholicism, which has particular rules about who is qualified to administer the Eucharist—the body and blood of Christ—there are few rules about who is qualified to lead the prayers in Islam. There is no ordination process, and any male can become the imam, which literally means the "person in front." Any Muslim male in uniform, in other words, could lead the prayers and give a brief sermon, which Hosein could even write. Leading the prayers is only a small part of a military chaplain's job, she rightly pointed out. A chaplain counsels service members of all faiths and no faith at all on personal issues and provides emotional and psychological support. A chaplain can teach about his or her religion and answer spiritual questions by relying on his or her expertise in that tradition. Hosein, who graduated from Hartford Seminary in 2007, possessed that expertise. But she was not able to fulfill her dream because of a military policy that remains in place.[21]

Still, Hosein remained in the military. She believed that her voice could make a difference for other Muslim service members, that she could continue to educate non-Muslims about Islam, and that she could do her part in bridging an ever widening divide between Muslims and non-Muslims in the contemporary world. Lt. Col. Hosein retired in 2014, leaving behind a thirty-five-year legacy of service to her adopted homeland.

Though Hosein's story is unique, it is also only one of thousands of similar stories of the children of Muslim immigrants. As the United States went to war against groups and nations that happened to be Muslim, many of these service members attempted to fight anti-Muslim stereotypes through their personal example of loyalty and bravery. Even if these Muslim service members mourned the Muslim enemies and innocents who were killed during these wars, they remained steadfast in their duty.

Notes

1. Sally Howell, "Federation of Islamic Associations of the United States and Canada," in *Encyclopedia of Muslim-American History*, ed. Edward E. Curtis IV (New York: Facts on File, 2010), 192–194.

2. Clinton Bennett, "United States Military," in *Encyclopedia of Muslim-American History*, ed. Edward E. Curtis IV (New York: Facts on File, 2010); and Harvey Ronald Stark, "Looking for Leadership: Discovering American Islam in the Muslim Chaplaincy," PhD diss., Princeton University, 2015, 229.

3. Dorothy Roberts, *Killing the Black Body: Race, Reproduction, and the Meaning of Liberty* (New York: Pantheon Books, 1997).

4. Coverage of the Nation of Islam is based on Edward E. Curtis IV, *Black Muslim Religion in the Nation of Islam, 1960–1975* (Chapel Hill: University of North Carolina Press, 2006).

5. Edward E. Curtis IV, *Islam in Black America* (Albany: State University of New York Press, 2002), 110.

6. Unless otherwise noted, my account of Muhammad Ali is from William Brown, "Muhammad Ali," in *Encyclopedia of Muslim-American History*, ed. Edward E. Curtis IV (New York: Facts on File, 2010), 40-44.

7. Associated Press, "Clay Says He Has Adopted Islam Religion and Regards It as Way to Peace," *New York Times*, February 28, 1964, https://www.nytimes.com/books/98/10/25/specials/ali-islam.html.

8. George C. Herring, *America's Longest War: The United States and Vietnam, 1950–1975*, 5th ed. (New York: McGraw Hill, 2014).

9. Associated Press. "In this April 28, 1967 file photo, heavyweight boxing champion Muhammad Ali is escorted from the Armed Forces Examining and Entrance Station in Houston by Lt. Col. J. Edwin McKee, commandant of the station, after Ali refused Army induction. Ali, the magnificent heavyweight champion whose fast fists and irrepressible personality transcended sports and captivated the world, has died according to a statement released by his family Friday, June 3, 2016. He was 74." © 2016 The Associated Press.

10. "Muhammad Ali Refuses to Fight in Vietnam," alpha history, http://alphahistory.com/vietnamwar/muhammad-ali-refuses-to-fight-1967.

11. Curtis, *Islam in Black America*, 116.

12. Lyndon Bilal, interview by author, August 15, 2016.

13. "Imam W. D. Mohammed at the Pentagon," YouTube video, 28:49, posted by "rodeoplaya," March 17, 2013, https://www.youtube.com/watch?v=zx_mQ4gDrgk; Stark, "Looking for Leadership," 240; and see also Jeff Diamant, "Engagement and Resistance: African Americans, Saudi Arabia and Islamic Transnationalisms, 1975 to 2000," PhD diss., City University of New York, 2016.

14. My account of Shakir's military service is from Zaid Shakir, *Scattered Pictures: Reflections of an American Muslim* (Hayward, CA: Zaytuna Institute, 2005), 16–18.

15. The coverage above of the Hart-Celler Act and Muslim American immigrants after 1965 is taken from Edward E. Curtis IV, *Muslims in America: A Short History* (New York: Oxford University Press), 72–94.

16. My account of Fatima Ahmed's service in the military is taken from my email correspondence with her on August 25–26, 2016.

17. Carlyle Murphy, "Soldier of Faith," *Washington Post Magazine,* January 20, 2008, http://www.washingtonpost.com/wp-dyn/content/article/2008/01/16/AR2008011603131.html.

18. The account above is from an interview with Shareda Hosein by David Washburn, April 25, 2016. Shareda Hosein also clarified various points with me via email and telephone on August 25, 2016.

19. Ibid.

20. Murphy, "Soldier of Faith."

21. Ibid. See also Stark, "Looking for Leadership."

FOUR

AFTER 9/11: SUSPICION, TRAGEDY, DUTY, AND LOVE IN AN AGE OF TERROR

MANY MUSLIM MEMBERS OF THE US MILITARY—and those who would be inspired to enlist in the military—vividly recall where they were on September 11, 2001, when members of al-Qaeda hijacked four airplanes and then turned them into weapons.[1] Nearly three thousand people were murdered as two planes brought down both towers of New York's World Trade Center and one jet crashed into the Pentagon, the headquarters for the Department of Defense. Still another hijacked plane crashed into a field in Pennsylvania.

If 9/11 changed US society as a whole, it had an even greater impact on Muslim Americans serving in and out of uniform. Al-Qaeda and its leader, Osama bin Laden, explained these attacks as retribution for what they considered to be US attacks on Muslims. The US government, it said, had unjustly defended corrupt regimes, including those of Kuwait and Saudi Arabia, throughout the Middle East; the United States supported the Israeli occupation of Palestinian lands; and the United States established "infidel" military bases in Islamic lands.

In response to the al-Qaeda attacks on September 11, 2001, President George W. Bush ordered US military forces to invade Afghanistan and remove the Taliban government that had permitted al-Qaeda to operate within its territory. This military action, which would include building a new national government, has been one of the United States' longest wars. The Taliban continues to fight US forces.

In 2003, President Bush ordered US military forces to also invade Iraq. While Iraq had nothing to do with the al-Qaeda attacks on 9/11, the

Bush administration said the Iraqi government posed a serious threat to US security. The US Congress authorized the military action based largely on the claim that Iraq had violated numerous United Nations resolutions by illegally producing weapons of mass destruction (WMDs), a claim that was later discovered to be incorrect. The Bush administration removed Iraqi president Saddam Hussein and disbanded the Iraqi army. An insurgency used the tools of asymmetrical warfare—car bombs, improvised explosive devices (IEDs), and the like—to oppose the US occupation, which officially ended in 2011.

These wars cost from \$1 to \$4 trillion and led to the deaths of hundreds of thousands of people. Thousands of US service members were killed, and tens of thousands injured. Many more troops would report suffering from post-traumatic stress disorder when they returned home.

Muslim American members of the military, and Muslims more generally, were right to worry that some Americans might develop anti-Muslim prejudices. The enemy in both Iraq and Afghanistan happened to be Muslim. And al-Qaeda had struck the United States in the name of Islam. After 9/11, hate crimes against Muslims soared by 1,600 percent.[2] Some Muslims—or those who "looked like" them such as Balbir Singh Sodhi, a Sikh—were murdered. Muslim women wearing headscarves were spat on. The US government detained about 1,200 Arab and Muslim men because they were suspected of ties to terrorism. "I thought we were going to be rounded up and put in Japanese-style internment camps," remembered PO First Class Fatima Ahmed, who was in the US Navy at the time. "I was terrified I'd be locked up."[3]

Those same suspicions were present in the US military. Ahmed remembered when she was fasting during the Islamic month of Ramadan, for example, one supervisor would order pizza and intentionally eat it in front of her. "The challenge," Ahmed told author Robin Wright, "was always being seen as if you didn't belong—and not knowing if people you interacted with didn't trust you, because of your religion."[4] After 9/11, Muslim American service members were on edge. "It's the feeling you can't be American enough—when you can't get more American than serving in the military. It's the raw hatred that some people have, out of complete ignorance. When they see ISIS, they think that's what Muslims are, what all of us are, which is incredibly wrong."[5] As Muslim army chaplain Dawud Agbere, originally from Ghana in West Africa, put it, "Are there some people in the military who think Muslims don't belong? I don't think you can run away from that."[6]

In the case of one man, US Army chaplain Capt. James Yee, such suspicions led to false accusations of treason. His persecution proved to some critics that the military was no place for a practicing Muslim. In another exceptional case, the worst fears of both Muslim and non-Muslim service members—that a Muslim member of the military would turn on his brothers- and sisters-in-arms—came true: Maj. Nidal Hasan murdered thirteen people in 2009 at Fort Hood.

These two cases have important lessons, but they are also exceptional. This chapter examines both cases, while also depicting the more typical and sometimes extraordinary service of Muslims who served in the military after 9/11. To be sure, anti-Muslim prejudice existed in the military, and some Muslim military members opposed the US wars in Afghanistan (2001) and Iraq (2003). But neither of these trends convinced large numbers of Muslim American military personnel to abandon their posts. To understand Muslim military service after 9/11, it is necessary to also tell the stories of soldiers, sailors, airmen, and marines who did not make the headlines.

CAPTAIN JAMES YEE, MUSLIM CHAPLAIN AT GUANTANAMO BAY

On September 10, 2003, Capt. James Yee, the Muslim chaplain at Camp Delta in Guantanamo Bay, Cuba, was arrested for mutiny, sedition, aiding the enemy, and espionage.[7]

It was a shocking turn of events for Yee, who was a graduate of the US Military Academy at West Point. A third-generation Chinese American, Yee came from a family with a history of military service. His father joined the US Army in 1945 and was posted to Seattle, Washington. One of Yee's brothers also attended West Point, and another brother joined the US Army as a physician.

Yee's path to becoming a Muslim chaplain began in 1991, when he converted from his childhood faith as a Lutheran to Islam just before being posted to Bitburg Air Base in Germany. There, Yee, who chose Yusuf as his Arabic name, was part of the air defense artillery, serving as platoon leader. On September 27, Yee was sent to Saudi Arabia. Saddam Hussein, still in power after the Gulf War ended in the removal of his forces from Kuwait, had refused some weapons inspectors' request to take documents from a nuclear design facility. Yee's job was to protect a Patriot missile system, the purpose of which was to intercept any Scud missiles that Hussein decided to launch.

Capt. James Yee, Muslim chaplain at Guantanamo Bay, was falsely accused of sedition in 2003 and was exonerated in 2004. (Credit Niccolo Caranti [CC Attribution-Share Alike 3.0] via Wikimedia Commons.)

When some Saudi airmen discovered that Yee and others serving at the King Abdulaziz Air Base were Muslims, they invited them to visit Mecca on an *umra*, a "lesser" pilgrimage performed outside of the time frame for the official hajj pilgrimage. In Mecca, Yee was deeply moved by the diversity of Muslim pilgrims there from all over the world, including the United States. It inspired him to seek more Islamic religious education.

Yee was less than fulfilled in his current military job, and the army was in the process of downsizing after the Gulf War. He was offered the chance to separate early from active duty and join the reserves. After working in the corporate world a little, Yee decided to pursue his dream of Islamic seminary education and eventually enrolled at the Abu Nour Islamic foundation in Damascus. Here, Yee was trained in the religious sciences of Islam, including the Qur'an; the hadith, which are reports of what the Prophet Muhammad said and did; and the Sharia, which are the Islamic legal and ethical teachings based on these sacred scriptures.

In the late 1990s, Yee became interested in rejoining the army—this time as a Muslim chaplain. On January 7, 2001, he reported for duty. After completing the basic course in chaplaincy, Yee was assigned to Fort Lewis, Washington. Yee ministered there to a small community of Muslims, but most of his work with the 730 military personnel on base was with non-Muslims. He spent a lot of his time counseling Christians and those without a formal religious affiliation on marital problems, grief, depression, and so on.

This is the job of a military chaplain, an institution that has been part of the US military since the American Revolution. It was Gen. George Washington who believed that spiritual guidance and pastoral care were necessary to military morale and success. The First Amendment to the US Constitution prohibits the federal government from establishing an official religion for the country, but the religious care of military personnel has always been seen as essential to the success of the military's mission. Plus, another section of the First Amendment guarantees the free exercise of religion for all individuals, no matter what their faith. A chaplain is supposed to help all members of the military, whether he or she shares the faith of the service member or not.[8]

Yee might have spent his entire career in this role had it not been for the terrorist attacks of 9/11. In the months following the attacks, the US government captured hundreds of people who, they said, may have had some connection to al-Qaeda, the Taliban rulers of Afghanistan, or other potential enemies of the United States. These detainees were not prisoners of war, claimed the government, but instead unlawful enemy combatants. The distinction was important since the government could argue that these enemy combatants were not entitled to full rights under the Geneva Conventions, which protect the basic well-being of all prisoners of war.

Instead of holding them in a regular military brig on US soil, where federal laws would govern their treatment, the US military set up a spe-

cial prison camp at Naval Station Guantanamo Bay, which was techni-
cally Cuban soil. In this legal no-man's-land, hundreds of detainees were
subjected to "enhanced interrogation techniques"—what some people
referred to as torture—in an attempt to gain information that might help
prevent a future attack on the United States. The government's position
was that it could keep these suspected combatants for as long as it wished.
It did not have to charge them with a crime or allow them to challenge
their detention in court.[9]

All of these men were Muslims, and in 2002, Yee was ordered to serve
as their chaplain.

When he arrived in Guantanamo, he was shocked by the horrible
conditions in which these men lived. They were put in "small cages" that
"measured eight feet by six feet and the prisoners shared a mesh wall
with two prisoners on each side." Only a tin roof protected from the el-
ements, and it worked to trap the hot Cuban air in the facility. They were
allowed showers only once every three days, and the smell in the stalls was
offensive.

Even more shocking to Yee, however, was the way that interrogators
and guards used religion to humiliate the detainees. During inspections
and interrogations, military personnel would regularly mishandle copies
of the Qur'an, tear out pages, break the bindings, throw the Qur'an on
the dirty floor, and even kick it across the stall. In some instances, guards
may have also written profanities and pasted pictures on some detainees'
copies of the Qur'an. Yee complained and was subsequently asked by base
commanders to develop standard operating procedures (SOPs) for han-
dling copies of the Qur'an. But the abuse of this sacred object did not stop.

Perhaps the charges filed against Yee were retribution for his speaking up about a culture of religious humiliation, or maybe it was because, as
he put it, he was "one of them"—that is, a Muslim. Whatever the reason,
the military arrested him.

He was held in solitary confinement in an eight-by-six cell at a Naval
Consolidated Brig in Charleston, South Carolina, for more than seventy
days. During this time, major media outlets reported, based on anony-
mous government sources, that Yee may have been part of an al-Qaeda spy
ring at Guantanamo. Senator Charles Schumer of New York, a Democrat,
wrote to Secretary of Defense Donald Rumsfeld, a Republican, that "the
successful infiltration of the Guantanamo Bay facility by Captain Yousef
[sic] Yee . . . indicates that enemies of the United States are continuing
their anti-American crusade."

Camp Delta at Guantanamo Bay, Cuba, was designed to hold Muslim "enemy combatants" who were not protected by the Geneva Conventions, according to the US government. (Photo by Kathleen T. Rhem.)

But weeks later, the military decided to charge Yee only with failing to safeguard classified material, an offense of which many US politicians, both Democrat and Republican, have themselves been guilty. Yee was released from prison and then charged with four other crimes, including adultery. Eventually, the military dropped the charges of mishandling classified evidence and reprimanded Yee for conduct unbecoming an officer. His military career was over, but he was honorably discharged and given an official commendation.

Yee was not the only service member at "Gitmo," as the military sometimes refers to Guantanamo Bay, who was harassed or wrongly suspected of disloyalty to his brothers- and sisters-in-arms. It is clear that in the post–9/11 era, many Muslim members of the military would feel the heat of anti-Islamic prejudice, including questions about their loyalty. It is all the more remarkable, then, that Muslim Americans have made such sacrifices to defend a nation-state in which a very basic aspect of their identity—their religion—has come under fire.

Some Muslims in the US military surely questioned whether the Iraq War was a sincere effort to reduce terrorism. At least 80 percent of Muslim Americans, like 40 percent or so of Americans more generally, opposed the war before it even began.[10] Even if they had questions, almost all of them put aside such concerns and did their duty.

But in at least one case, a Muslim soldier became so opposed to the wars in Iraq and Afghanistan, and he feared being posted to Afghanistan so much, that he lashed out violently. That man was Maj. Nidal Hasan.

MAJOR NIDAL HASAN

On November 5, 2009, US Army Maj. Nidal Hasan, dressed in a military uniform, pointed two handguns at fellow soldiers at a medical processing center at Fort Hood, Texas, and started firing. By the time he finished, Hasan had murdered thirteen people and injured thirty more.[11]

Hasan, an army psychiatrist, was born 1970 in Arlington, Virginia. His parents, restauranteurs, were Palestinian immigrants who came from a small town outside of Jerusalem. They expressed reservations about their son joining the US armed forces after he graduated from high school. Young Hasan told them, "I was born and raised here. I'm going to do my duty to the country."[12]

After attending West Virginia Northern Community College and Virginia Tech, Hasan became an officer in the Army Medical Department in 1997. He completed psychiatry training at Uniformed Services University of the Health Sciences in Bethesda, Maryland, in 2003. Neither of his parents would get to share that accomplishment with him. His father died in 1998, and his mother passed away in 2001. Though he apparently looked to get married, he never found a suitable mate. Hasan finished his medical residency at Walter Reed Army Medical Center in Washington, DC, in 2007. In 2009, he was posted to Fort Hood, where, by all accounts, he kept mostly to himself.[13]

Throughout his medical training and residence, Hasan was troubled by the anti-Muslim prejudice that he witnessed in both his patients and fellow soldiers. As early as 2004, he complained about the presence of Islamophobia in the military to his relatives. Though she was speaking in general, perhaps retired Lt. Col. Shareda Hosein's analysis of Muslim American life after 9/11 applied to Hasan:

> A lot of Muslims experience moral injury in the military. We are Muslims, and, whether we self-identify or not, our country calls us to defend the nation, including everyone's freedom of religion. Yet internally we have this sense that they don't want us. And there's a degree of harassment. So many of us experience a form of P.T.S.D. because of a feeling we are not considered equal to our colleagues. This emotional wound is something far greater, because you can't verbalize it. No one wants to know.[14]

Hasan was questioning his choice to become a military doctor. The stories that his patients told him about the terrible things they had done to Muslims in Iraq and Afghanistan disturbed him. And in 2009, he was about to be posted to Afghanistan. "He was mortified by the idea of having to deploy," his cousin said. "He had people telling him on a daily basis the horrors they saw over there."[15]

Hasan treated patients with severe psychiatric trauma related to military service. This included service members from Iraq and Afghanistan who had either attempted suicide or were thinking about it. "The worst we saw were the patients who had shot themselves in the head or face and survived," remembered Lt. Eric Notkin, a nurse who helped treat patients with Hasan at Walter Reed.[16]

Hasan's area of research interest focused on the conflicts that Muslim soldiers might have in serving in these wars, a conflict that he shared. In a presentation given to medical colleagues at Walter Reed in 2007, Hasan, soft-spoken, calm, and perhaps even sullen, asserted that the Qur'an forbids Muslims from killing other Muslims and that this fact, by definition, produced a potential conflict inside of the American Muslim soldier.

His PowerPoint presentation, which was fifty slides long, made a complex argument for those unfamiliar with Islamic religion. It included basic information about Muslims and Islamic religion but also broached more complicated topics such as Islamic law and ethics. According to Hasan, most Islamic legal scholars outside the United States tended to forbid the participation of Muslims in the US military, while scholars in the United States permitted it. He noted, however, that Islamic legal rulings were ambiguous, and he encouraged legal scholars to make clear exactly what Muslim soldiers could or could not do. No one, for example, denied the right of a Muslim to capture bin Laden. But making general war in Afghanistan and Iraq was a different matter. Hasan spent significant time during the presentation giving his own reading of Qur'anic verses concerning God's demand of complete obedience, the rewards of heaven and the punishment of hell, and war and peace. He included the verses that encourage military attacks on unbelievers until they submit to Islamic political authority, noting that the verse is "uncomfortable for many Muslims." He also argued that the Qur'an makes clear that Islam is the only acceptable religion in God's eyes.[17]

Hasan asserted that the establishment of an Islamic state is an obligation on all Muslims. Because the Muslim American soldier is caught between his religion and his country, he concluded, conscientious objector status should be available to all Muslims in the military who share this point of view. Afterward, some of his colleagues were shocked and angry, accusing Hasan of radical views. Others thought it a "useful analysis of the dueling pressures on Muslims in the American military."[18]

During the question-and-answer portion of the presentation, one man asked what was probably the most important question of the day. He queried whether mental health care professionals "should be telling commanders and health care providers that anyone who is a practicing Muslim is someone we should keep an eye on and be aware of?"

"Yeah, absolutely sensitive issue," Hasan responded. "You're right. I'm not sure how to maneuver over that. You're right."[19]

It was a question that Hasan could never answer. For him, there seemed to be no answer. He was in a no-win situation.

Perhaps his shooting rampage was his only way out. In the years after the shooting, mental health care professionals reminded those worried about other Muslim American service members that a crisis of conscience does not necessarily lead a person toward anti-social behavior.[20] Moral dilemmas are part of the human experience, and most of us find better ways to deal with them.[21] Many other psychological factors seemed important to understanding why Hasan chose this form of protest over more constructive ones. Some critics said that Hasan was just another Muslim terrorist. But that explanation was too simplistic. It ignored the complex humanity of this soldier who did such an awful thing. Even if Hasan was acting on the idea that the US military was fighting an unjust war against all Muslims, his case suggests that psychological problems and the trauma he had experienced played roles in his decision making.

It seems that Hasan did have a death wish—an idea that he discussed in his 2007 presentation. When he was brought before a military court martial for his murders, Hasan insisted on defending himself. The result was predictable. The jury decided to end his life by lethal injection, an earthly punishment that awaits this soldier pending judicial appeals.

LANCE CORPORAL ABRAHAM AL-THAIBANI

For some, the story of Hasan is a cautionary tale of what can happen when soldiers with conflicting loyalties serve in the US military. The story has resonance because it confirms the prejudicial and powerful notion that Muslims are somehow inherently un-American. Alternate narratives, like the one of Capt. Humayun Khan, come to the public's attention only on rare occasions. It might seem that for every Khan, there is one Hasan, but this would be incorrect. There are hundreds of stories of Muslim Americans deployed in Iraq and Afghanistan who have seen the deaths of both insurgents and civilians and yet continue to serve with courage.

The story of L. Cpl. Abraham Al-Thaibani, told by author and attorney Alia Malek in *A Country Called Amreeka*, illustrates the steadfast nature of nearly all Muslims in the US armed services.[22] Al-Thaibani's parents arrived from the country of Yemen in 1968, and though his father had been a police officer in Qatar, he took a job as an elevator operator in New York. Al-Thaibani, who was born in the United States, attended New York Public School 142 in Lower Manhattan. During the Gulf War (1990–1991), kids at his school teased him, saying, "We're going to kick your Arab ass." Al-Thaibani fought back, leading to suspension from school, but he also vowed that he would join the military so that someone would tie a yellow ribbon around a tree for him. He was twelve years old.

In 1998, after graduating from John Dewey High School in Brooklyn, Al-Thaibani enlisted in the US Marine Corps Reserve. He believed in freedom, and he wanted to do his part. He married Esmihan, and they had a son named Farid. Al-Thaibani was going full time to John Jay College of Criminal Justice and also working, like his father, as an elevator operator. After 9/11, he was called up for duty.

A member of the Second Battalion, Twenty-Fifth Marines, known as the Empire Battalion, Al-Thaibani was trained as a rifleman. But the Marine Corps assigned him to counterintelligence in Iraq because he was fluent in Arabic. Working in the city of Nasiriyah in 2003, Al-Thaibani helped with interrogations of prisoners or persons of interest, went on raids, and worked undercover. His team captured Nagem Sadoon Hatab, a former Saddam Hussein loyalist who may have been involved in the capture of Pvt. Jessica Lynch's convoy. Hatab was detained and perhaps beaten at Camp Whitehorse until a marine removed him from his cell and left him to die in the Iraqi sun. Two marines were charged and acquitted of crimes related to the incident. Al-Thaibani testified at the trial saying that he had witnessed no abuse when he had been in the presence of the detainee. The prosecutors were only interested in "crucifying the Marines," Al-Thaibani added. Looking back on it years later, Al-Thaibani stressed the importance of loyalty to one fellow's marines. "You went together and you come home together."[23]

This was not the only incident in Iraq when Al-Thaibani's conscience would be tested. On April 11, 2003, less than a month after the US forces had invaded Iraq, calls of "shots fired!" and "civilians hurt!" poured out of Al-Thaibani's radio. The calls were coming from Echo Company of the Second Battalion, Twenty-Fifth Marines—his platoon. When Al-Thaibani and his partner arrived at the scene on the Saddam Canal bridge in Nasiriyah, Al-Thaibani saw blood, glass, and a passenger van destroyed by gunfire. The scene was gruesome. A man crying out for help. A woman howling. A boy who had been hit. A doctor tending to another woman.

And the bodies of two little children—two girls, it turned out—swathed in plastic camouflage.

Al-Thaibani took another look at the howling woman, as he cried out, "Who's shot?" He discovered that she was holding a baby boy. He seemed lifeless. But the boy had just fainted, the doctor told him.

"Why did you kill my babies?" she moaned.

The shooting was an accident. The family's passenger van had not seen the signs that indicated, in Arabic and with pictures, to stop. They had not heard the guards' commands either. And the guards, who were looking straight into the sun, could not see who was in the van.

An ambulance arrived, and Al-Thaibani tried to convince the woman, whose lung had been shot, to go for medical treatment. She resisted, finally screaming to him, "You should be ashamed of yourself. You are Arab! You are coming to an Arab country to kill Arabs!"[24]

Al-Thaibani was sad. During the rest of his tour, he tried to help Iraqi civilians, especially children, in any way that he could. He advocated for them at the base hospital where it was rare for Iraqi civilians to be treated for their normal healthcare needs. He applied first aid himself when he could not get them in to see an American doctor. When he wanted to unwind, Al-Thaibani, accompanied by his partner, would drive far out in the desert to spend time with the Bedouin, the semi-nomadic people who live in durable, spacious tents. Sitting on a carpet, his back against some pillows, he spent hours listening to old songs about the glories of Iraq, one of the world's first civilizations. His hosts asked questions about America, and they fed him lamb, fish, and bread.

Al-Thaibani returned home in August 2013. He felt proud of his service. "When he enlisted," wrote Malek, "he always knew that there was a possibility he would one day face soldiers that were Arab like himself." He did not permit himself to think too much about it. He would deal with it when it happened. And he did his duty while also doing his best to help Iraqi civilians: "The war would have happened regardless if he were there or not; his presence, Abraham realized, guided by trying to do something right, had served a purpose."[25]

MAJOR JAMES AHEARN

Though the wars in Iraq and Afghanistan resulted in millions of personal tragedies, other aspects of the human experience did not disappear completely in the ruins of war. Love, even romantic love, sometimes grew from the scorched ground of these two countries.

Born in 1963, Maj. James Ahearn joined the military in 1989. He served in a tank crew during the Gulf War, and then in 1994, he graduated from Officer Candidate School at Fort Benning, Georgia. Joining the Twenty-Seventh Engineer Brigade, Ahearn was posted over the following years to Fort Stewart, Georgia, and Fort Irwin National Training Center, California.[26]

In 2003, Ahearn was sent to Iraq. He met Lena when he knocked on a door in one of the neighborhoods that he was assigned to patrol.[27] A university graduate with a degree in psychology, she was the only person in her house who spoke English. Her mother woke her up so that she could talk to Ahearn.

It was love at first sight.

"Those blue eyes!" Lena remembered. "Oh, man, he has beautiful white teeth! And he has the strong officer face."

At eight o'clock that very evening, Ahearn returned to the house to ask Lena is she would like to chat.

Lena's brother chaperoned the couple as they repeated the same ritual night after night for a month. Sitting on a bench, they spent hours in conversation. They joked with one another and they flirted. They fell in love.

Ahearn asked her to marry him. But Lena was Muslim. And so, if he wanted to marry her, he would have to convert to Islam.

Lena told him, "I only want you to convert if you believe in it."[28]

They wed in Jordan, the country located to the west of Iraq. The more difficult step was getting Lena to the United States. To do that, Ahearn asked for the help of his father, the former head of the FBI office in Phoenix, and Arizona senator John McCain, a decorated air force pilot and former prisoner of war.

The couple reprised their wedding for American friends and family in Las Vegas, Nevada. Lena wore a wedding gown and dyed her hair blonde for the occasion.

They moved near Fort Bragg, South Carolina, where Ahearn served with the Ninety-Sixth Civil Affairs Battalion. They had a daughter named Khadijah, whom they called Kadi.

Two years after marrying Lena, "Jimmy," as she called him, still acted like a newlywed. Every Sunday morning he would buy Lena a flower and a card, sometimes hiding them around the house. "He put them on top of refrigerator," she said, "inside the refrigerator beside the milk where I have my coffee creamer, in the cabinet, in the kitchen. In the laundry room. Whenever I open my draw[er]. When I go to the bathroom, I brush my teeth I found one on the mirror."[29]

In 2007, Ahearn was posted to Iraq for the third time. His goal was to help residents in various neighborhoods work together to increase local security. Four years after the US invasion, Iraq remained in perilous condition. Ahearn wrote an email to his father explaining that detonation of car bombs and other acts of terrorism directed toward civilians were meant to tear Iraqi society apart. On April 22, he said, one neighborhood was attacked because of its religious and ethnic diversity:

> A common technique is to commit some random act of violence as a catalyst for sectarian infighting, after which either the Sunnis or Shia come out on top. There are now large swathes of Baghdad which are homogenous as a result . . . Anyway, these people reacted differently. This neighborhood (Sunni, Shia, Christian and Kurd) came together. They cared for the injured, put up the homeless, built makeshift barriers around the neighborhood to prevent such a thing from happening again.[30]

Ahearn was committed to supporting these efforts and was willing to risk his life to do so.

On his way to a community meeting on July 5, 2007, his truck was hit by a roadside bomb, and Ahearn was killed.

After a memorial service at Fort Bragg, Ahearn was given an Islamic burial service at Arlington National Cemetery. Lena was devastated. She wrote love letters to him on Internet memorial sites, and she and Kadi moved to Virginia, not far from Ahearn's grave. It was especially hard when Kadi would look at a picture of her father and say, "Baba"—Arabic for *daddy*.

Lena sought solace among other widows of war veterans, though she was worried they might not accept her.

"If you guys don't like me," she said, "for whatever reason, I totally understand."

They responded by hugging her.

Soon after, Lena joined some of her fellow widows in a skydiving trip. "Jimmy was airborne so I really wanted to know what it felt like, what he did. That night I did it, I had an amazing dream, like he came to me and he was still alive."[31]

Ahearn's memory lived on not only in the hearts of his family members but also in the growing consciousness of a public that was beginning to take note of Muslim Americans in uniform.

The years after 9/11 were unprecedented. US military personnel, including Muslims, had battled foreign Muslims before—in the Southern Philippines (1899–1913), in Lebanon in both 1958 and 1982, in Kuwait in 1991. But this was different. After 9/11, an increasing number of Americans both inside and outside the military thought that the enemy was not simply people who were Muslim, but the Islamic religion itself. This fear of Islam sometimes drove US military personnel to make rash decisions, like when they too quickly suspected Capt. James Yee of treason. The suspicion toward Muslims and Islam also increased the sense of fear, even dread, among American service members who were Muslim. In spite of this difficult environment, Muslim American service members did their duty in the wars in Iraq and Afghanistan. Even if they sometimes questioned the policy decisions that drove these wars, Muslim Americans were willing to make the ultimate sacrifice, and some of them did.

Notes

1. My account of 9/11 and its aftermath is based on Edward E. Curtis IV, *Muslims in America: A Short History* (New York: Oxford University Press, 2009).

2. Curt Andersen, "FBI: Hate Crimes vs. Muslims Rise," *Associated Press*, November 25, 2002, http://www.apnewsarchive.com/2002/FBI-Hate-Crimes-Vs-Muslims-Rise/id-5e249fb6e4dc184720e3428c9d0bd046.

3. Robin Wright, "Humayun Khan Isn't the Only Muslim American Hero," *New Yorker*, August 15, 2016, http://www.newyorker.com/news/news-desk/humayun-khan-isnt-the-only-muslim-american-hero.

4. Ibid.

5. Ibid.

6. Jennifer H. Svan, "Muslims in Military Say 'Everybody Belongs,'" *Stars and Stripes*, Sept. 16, 2007, http://www.stripes.com/news/muslims-in-military-say-everybody-belongs-1.68856.

7. Unless otherwise noted, all material on James Yee is based on James Yee with Aimee Moloy, *For God and Country: Faith and Patriotism under Fire* (New York: Public Affairs, 2005).

8. Harvey Ronald Stark, "Looking for Leadership: Discovering American Islam in the Muslim Chaplaincy," PhD diss., Princeton University, 2015, 217–229.

9. Diana Coleman, "Guantanamo Bay," in *Encyclopedia of Muslim-American History*, ed. Edward E. Curtis IV (New York: Facts on File, 2010), 219–221.

10. Andrea Elliott, "Sorting Out Life as Muslims and Marines," *New York Times*, Aug. 7, 2006.

11. Robert D. McFadden, "Army Doctor Held in Ft. Hood Rampage," *New York Times*, Nov. 5, 2009.

12. "The Life and Career of Major Hasan," *New York Times*, November 6, 2009.

13. Ibid.

14. As quoted in Robin Wright, "Humayun Khan Isn't the Only Muslim American Hero."

15. James Dao, "Suspect Was 'Mortified' about Deployment," *New York Times*, Nov. 5, 2009.

16. Nidal Hasan, "The Koranic World View as It Relates to Muslims in the U.S. Military," Fox News video, 17:27, posted September 10, 2013, http://video.foxnews .com/v/2663135028001/nidal-hasans-june-2007-grand-rounds-presentation-part -1/?#sp=show-clips; Scott Shane and James Dao, "Investigators Study Tangle of Clues on Fort Hood Suspect," *New York Times*, Nov. 14, 2009.

17. Hasan, "Koranic World View as It Relates to Muslims in the U.S. Military."

18. Ibid.; Shane and Dao, "Investigators Study Tangle of Clues on Fort Hood Suspect."

19. Hasan, "Koranic World View As It Relates to Muslims in the U.S. Military."

20. Wahiba Abu-Ras et al., "Addressing Mental Health Issues among American Muslims in the Military," Institute for Social Policy and Understanding, June 2010, http://www.ispu.org/pdfs/ISPU-MentalHealth_Report.pdf.

21. For one of the very few studies on mental health and religion of Muslim Americans in the military, see Wahiba Abu-Ras, "Understanding Resiliency through Vulnerability: Cultural Meaning and Religious Practice among Muslim Military Personnel," *Psychology of Religion and Spirituality* 7, no. 3 (2015): http://dx .doi.org/10.1037/rel0000017.

22. All quotations and facts for this section, unless otherwise noted, are based on Alia Malek, *A Country Called Amreeka: Arab Roots, American Stories* (New York: Free Press, 2009), 243–259.

23. Elliott, "Sorting Out Life as Muslims and Marines."

24. Malek, *A Country Called Amreeka*, 250.

25. Ibid., 258.

26. Quoted in "James Michael Ahearn," Arlington National Cemetery Website, http://arlingtoncemetery.net/jmahearn.htm.

27. My account of Lena meeting James, including the quotations, unless otherwise noted, is from Petula Dvorak, "An Unlikely Love Story amid the Casualties of War in Iraq," *Sydney Morning Herald*, May 30, 2010, http://www.smh.com.au/world /an-unlikely-love-story-amid-the-casualties-of-war-in-iraq-20100529-wmme.html.

28. Quoted in "James Michael Ahearn," Arlington National Cemetery Website, http://arlingtoncemetery.net/jmahearn.htm.

29. Ibid.

30. Ibid.

31. Dvorak, "An Unlikely Love Story amid the Casualties of War in Iraq."

FIVE

TODAY'S MUSLIM AMERICANS IN UNIFORM

TODAY'S MUSLIM MEMBERS OF THE MILITARY reflect the remarkable ethnic and racial diversity of the Muslim American communities from which they come. Among Muslim Americans generally, no single racial group accounts for the majority. According to the Gallup polling organization, "Muslims are the only religious group [in the United States] to lack a majority race or ethnicity, with 36% self-identifying as non-Hispanic black, 27% as non-Hispanic white, 21% as Asian and 8% as Hispanic."[1] The Muslim American military community is similar in its make-up. The largest single racial group of Muslim service members identify themselves as black; this includes American-born people of African descent and African-born people who have emigrated from sub-Saharan Africa. Other Muslim members of military may identify their race as white, Asian, or Hispanic. As this book has already revealed, many of them trace their roots to the Middle East, North Africa, and South Asia.[2] But there are also Muslim service members who have roots in Latin America and the Caribbean, Europe, East Asia, Central Asia, and Southeast Asia.

More than five thousand service members in the US Army, Navy, Air Force, and Marines—both active duty and reserves—have registered as Muslim with the Department of Defense. Because almost half a million service members have not expressed a religious preference, there are likely many more Muslims or people from a Muslim background serving in uniform. Perhaps ten thousand more.[3] What the estimate does not include are the thousands, perhaps tens of thousands who have separated or retired from the military. These service members include hundreds, if not thousands, of women. Past estimates have stated that women may account for 10 percent or so of the total number of Muslims in the military.[4]

Muslim Americans constitute just 1–2 percent of the total US population. They likely compose an ever smaller percentage of military service members. But they play vital roles in the US military. This chapter provides the stories of the everyday lives of Muslim military service members, how they observe Islamic religious practices in the military, and what exactly it is that they do. As anyone who has served in the military will tell you, military service is not always high drama. It can be boring, just like every other job. But to understand Muslim military service, like the service of non-Muslims, we need to focus on the typical. Thus, these stories represent the ordinary experiences of Muslim military members.

Master Sergeant Laura Magee, Chaplain's Assistant

"For the previous fifteen years, I have dutifully served my nation and my local community as a member of the 152nd Airlift Wing," wrote M.Sgt. Laura Magee in the *High Roller News*, the newsletter of her Nevada Air National Guard unit in Reno.[5] "I've always been proud of my calling, proud of my brothers and sisters in arms." But after spending fifteen years in the Air National Guard, something happened in her unit that made her re-evaluate her "pride in belonging to a prestigious military organization." Something wonderful happened, and it made Magee feel even more strongly attached to the military. "I belong to so much more than that [an organization]," she declared. "I belong to a family, and I could not be more proud!"

Magee asked permission to wear a head scarf as part of her uniform, and Col. Karl Stark, commander of the 152nd Airlift Wing, approved. "I asked to add a scarf to cover my head and neck," she said. "Yep, you read that correctly," she wrote for an audience of fellow airmen. "I did. I know . . . it was crazy." But then Stark not only granted her permission to wear a head scarf. He said that anyone under his command could do so for religious reasons.

Stark's approval applied only to indoor spaces on the base, meaning Magee was not permitted to wear a head scarf outdoors on base, a decision that would require more negotiations with military authorities. But Magee was elated—not only for herself but for the military overall. In her view, accommodating the religious practices of armed service members would strengthen morale and commitment.

"Religious accommodation," she wrote "is not a force divider; it is a forcer multiplier!" Magee asserted that the decision would reassure other religious people, no matter what their religion, that they would not have to

In 2016, M.Sgt. Laura Magee, chaplain assistant with the 152nd Airlift Wing in Reno, Nevada, was granted permission to wear a headscarf indoors while on base. (Photo by Mario Diaz.)

"sacrifice the religious beliefs that they hold so dearly." The decision would be especially helpful in recruiting women to the military, she stressed, since they would be able to serve their country while also maintaining their religious commitments to modesty in both dress and behavior.

Other women have requested permission to wear a head scarf in various units of the US military and have often been told no. Alterations in the uniform are especially taboo in military culture. This and all other religious accommodations inside the US military must take into account the effect of the accommodation on the service member's performance and safety as well as its impact on unit morale and cohesion. "We need to operate as a seamless, well-oiled machine," Magee stated, "not as a hodgepodge of random parts, each doing what it wants rather than what the machine requires." The military allows Jewish, Sikh, and Muslim men to wear some form of headgear in uniform, but according to Magee, wearing a female head scarf "is arguably a bit more extreme."

In 2014, Magee converted from Christianity to Islam.[6] Magee was not brought up to be a Christian, but even as a young girl, she prayed to God on her own. Her father, who was not religious at the time, "encouraged us to seek our own truths, to look for our own answers, but did not speak highly of religion." As a teenager, Magee continued to pray and studied the Bible on her own. After enlisting in the military, she attended Sunday church services; it was far better, she said, than "a day of folding underwear." In the meantime, her father had returned to his childhood faith of Christianity. She decided to get baptized and confessed that her Lord and Savior was Jesus Christ. Over time, however, she came to question this belief. She began to think that all religions ultimately worshipped God, and she could not accept the belief that Jesus was God or the belief that the Bible was the word of God.

Magee met a Muslim imam at Fort Jackson, South Carolina, in April 2014. As she learned about his religious journey, she was struck by a parallel between her own beliefs and his. And then she heard the first chapter of the Qur'an, called *al-Fatiha*, the Opening. "At the time the words were nothing but sounds, words in an unfamiliar language," she stated, "Yet at that same moment, they spoke to me . . . they spoke to my heart and soul."

Magee then read the entire Qur'an. She made notes and asked the imam about various verses. In the privacy of her room, she prostrated her body in the direction of Mecca two or three times a day. She read the Qur'an more. She discovered that "the words that He [God] has written on my heart were indeed reflected in His revelation." She formally became a Muslim in June of that year.

Some people in her life disapproved, and others celebrated her decision.[7] When some of her friends heard secondhand, they were upset that she had not told them directly. "I felt like I was admitting some horrible crime or social taboo," she later recalled. "Come to think of it, I kinda was. It is indeed taboo to embrace something at the center of so much controversy: Islam, of all religions, and *now*, of all the times in history." She was aware of the "toxic fear running through the nation's social veins." Certain people in her life were "appalled" that she became a Muslim.

Her brother used the image of Magee doing a cannonball into a swimming pool, the waves crashing up against people in their shared social world. Some of her relationships could not withstand the stress, though Magee still holds out hope for the possibility of reconciliation.

For her, it felt like a coming out, which she described as revealing "a truth about yourself that has always been there, always been an intimate part of who you are, but the signs of which people did not see or perhaps chose not to acknowledge." She said that the purpose of being public about her Muslim identity was not to get others to agree with her, but simply to let "the real you shine though."

As a chaplain's assistant in the 152nd Airlift Wing, Magee tends to the spiritual needs of service members who, generally speaking, do not share her faith. According to a 2015 survey conducted by the base Chaplains Corps, two-thirds of the base population identified as either Protestant or Catholic "followed in descending order by agnostic, atheist, Muslim, Wiccan/Pagan, Buddhist, Mormon, Jewish, Hindu, and Orthodox." In response to their requests, the Chaplain Corps pledged to help arrange for prayer time on base, scriptural studies for various religious groups, social activities such as BBQs and retreats, and a weekly Chaplain's Chat that would include a series on world religions.[8] Like other personnel in the Chaplains Corps, Magee also tries to support fellow airmen though the rigors of military life, including the stress of Unit Effectiveness Inspections.[9]

The service of Magee confronts a lot of stereotypes about Muslims and Islam in the military. Her case shows that you can be a Muslim who is completely committed to Islamic doctrine and still provide pastoral care to those who do not share your views. It reminds us that white people and women also convert to Islam in the military, despite the fact that their friends and family may not always support that choice. Her base commander's flexibility on wearing a head scarf also demonstrates the possibilities of greater religious accommodations within the US military as a whole.

The next story reveals that same openness to religious accommodations in the military. The main difference is that the commanding officer is himself a Muslim.

COLONEL NASHID SALAHUDDIN

Col. Nashid Salahuddin is the commander of the 175th Mission Support Group at Warfield Air National Guard Base in Maryland. He is in command of 450 airmen and oversees "civil engineering, security, supply, transportation, fuels, contracting, and communications supporting 1,400 members assigned to the 175th Wing" of the Maryland Air National Guard.[10]

The fact that Salahuddin is not a household name indicates how the everyday service of US Muslims is often unsung in the post–9/11 era.

Born in 1971 and raised a Muslim in New Orleans, Louisiana, Salahuddin came from a family that followed Elijah Muhammad and then his son, Imam W. D. Mohammed. After graduating from high school,

Col. Nashid Salahuddin is the commander of the 175th Mission Support Group at Warfield Air National Guard Base in Maryland. (Courtesy of Colonel Nashid Salahuddin.)

Salahuddin enrolled at Southern University and A&M College in Baton Rouge, Louisiana. But his first year of college was tough. "I joined the military, to be honest, because I didn't do that well my first year of college at Southern University," Salahuddin said in an interview. Salahuddin knew about the military because some of his cousins served in the navy and the marine corps. After speaking with recruiters from a couple branches of the armed forces, he decided to join the Air Force Reserve Command on active duty. "It was the best career decision that I've made in my life," he said. "I got to travel and I was exposed to the world. The military paid for my education."

After enlisting in 1990, Salahuddin completed his bachelor's degree in workforce education at Southern Illinois University. He entered officer training school in 1996 and served as an officer in the support flight group of the 159th Fighter Wing of the Louisiana National Guard in New Orleans. Salahuddin also worked in private industry in the field of human resources and technology, and in 2010, he received his master's degree from the New Jersey Institute of Technology in information systems.

In 2011, then Lt. Col. Salahuddin was deployed to Iraq. It would be his most memorable and meaningful experience in the military, "the biggest accomplishment of my twenty-five years in the Air Force." Salahuddin was assigned senior advisor to the Iraqi Ministry of Interior. His mission was to help strengthen border security. As part of Operation New Dawn, Salahuddin's job was more like corporate consulting than soldiering.

Assigned to the Ports of Entry Directorate, which is akin to the US Customs and Border Protection, Salahuddin helped standardize systems and procedures at eighteen different sites. The goal was to curb corruption and the illegal flow of arms and drugs across Iraqi borders.

"I felt like I was uniquely qualified to this job," he explained. Using skills gained from Six Sigma, a popular, statistic-driven quality management system, in addition to planning software and customer satisfaction surveys, Salahuddin offered advice on how Iraqi officials could meet their own goals for better security, more efficient collection of tariffs, and the smooth flow of both goods and people across the border. In order to stem corruption, Salahuddin's team advised that the government use a system of incentives for customs officials.

Since he was Muslim, Salahuddin said that he found it easy to work with senior Iraqi officials. "Because I was already familiar with their religion, I was able to connect on a personal level," he remembered. What he learned was that Iraqi Muslims "wanted the same basic things that all people want: basic security, education for their children, and jobs." Some of his Iraqi colleagues called him "Abu Rayan," the father of Rayan, his first-born son. In Iraq, like in some other Arabic-speaking countries, doing so is a sign of both respect and familiarity.

Salahuddin leaned on his faith in Iraq in other ways, too. "Even though the war was officially over," he explained, "the insurgents were not always aware of that fact." He had to travel through areas where there was fighting. Improvised explosive devices (IEDs), which had been one of the main threats to the US occupation of Iraq, were still a problem. Thirteen IEDs were detonated in an area that he had to visit the very next day. "I was afraid," he said, emphatically, "but this is when faith helped me. I prayed to Allah to help me through this situation. Whether you are Jewish, Christian, Muslim or something else, you need your faith in challenging circumstances like this."

On April 18, 2016, Salahuddin was promoted to the rank of colonel, and he assumed command of the 175th Mission Support Group.

As Salahuddin has climbed the military ranks, practicing Islam has become easier. "My experience as a Muslim is that the more senior you are, the easier it is to practice your faith," he said. "At my current rank I don't have to seek permission to attend *juma* [Friday congregational prayers]. I just go." It has not always been this easy for him. "When I was more junior," he said, "it was not always possible for me to follow Islamic dietary rules. One time, for example, I asked to have a food stipend rather than eating at the chow hall so that I could purchase my food off base. This request was denied." Now Salahuddin tries to accommodate the religious practices of those under his command: "I reach out to service members who may have a different religious background—like one Sikh Airman under my command—to see if they need anything."

As a religious minority of high rank, Salahuddin is the living embodiment of the promise that the US military does not discriminate on the basis of a service member's religion. But his success and the fact that he is a Muslim commander means even more. It shows that the military will advance the careers of a population some Americans distrust or fear. This is also the case with S.Sgt. Jibril Smythe, who handles some of the most sensitive intelligence in the country.

STAFF SERGEANT JIBRIL SMYTHE

Jibril Smythe is a staff sergeant for the US Army Intelligence and Security Command (INSCOM).[11] His work concerns computers and satellites, though he can't be more specific with me. Being a part of army intelligence and the National Security Agency at Fort George G. Meade, the home of "cyber warriors," requires discretion.

Smythe began his army career in 2010. A native of a Midwestern city, he was raised as a Muslim. Smythe completed both his bachelor's and master's degrees, and was working as a medical device salesperson when he decided to join. "I never felt like my job mattered," he told me. "I always felt like I was making money for someone else. I wanted to make a difference, to do something important."

Smythe pointed out that people can't walk off the street and do what he does. "The work that my team does has saved lives or prevented something bad from happening." Smythe is particularly proud of the time that one of his reports ended up in the president's daily brief, which is a top-secret summary of the most important security threats and other intelligence facing the US government on any given day.

I asked him whether it was hard practicing Islam in the military. "I work with a bunch of enlightened individuals," he said. When he served time in Korea, Smythe said, his supervisor was an Arabic linguist. "It was funny because when he spoke with me, he would regularly end his statements with the word *inshallah*" (an Arabic term meaning "God willing"). Then, when Smythe was posted to Fort Meade, his supervisor was yet another Arabic linguist, who had a deep knowledge of Islam.

Smythe thinks that for many of his fellow soldiers, his Muslim identity is invisible. "When people see me," he opined, "they see a black dude, black guy." His comment speaks to the widespread association of Islam after 9/11 with brown people who are perceived to be of Middle Eastern or South Asian descent. I pointed out that in the era of Muhammad Ali's tangle with the military, the face of Islam was black, not brown. But after 9/11, that changed.

"I remember in basic training that our First Sergeant would go on and on about hajjis, and I had no idea what he was talking about." As the stories of camel driver Hadji Ali and World War II veteran John Omar demonstrate, the term *hajji* is one of respect for someone who has completed the Islamic pilgrimage to Mecca. But during the post–9/11 wars, it became a label for all Muslims, and was sometimes used as an epithet.

Muslim identity, in other words, increasingly became a racial, rather than religious identity for some non-Muslims, and Smythe's blackness did not fit the stereotype.

It is important to him that fellow soldiers see him as Muslim because it is often the first time that they have ever worked alongside a Muslim. They see that Smythe has the same thoughts, the same feelings, as they do. "Some of them come from small towns, and they see that their supervisor is a Muslim, and he's just like anyone else—except he's just Muslim." Smythe said he "enjoyed debunking some of the stereotypes that people have."

Smythe told me that it is difficult to keep to a regular prayer sched-ule—for example, he is supposed to be at physical training at the same time he is supposed to perform the morning prayers. But Smythe often makes up his prayers when he gets home from work at the end of the day. He attends Friday congregational prayers when he has days off from work at a local mosque. Overall, military life does not conflict in any significant way with Smythe's religious commitments. If anything, his work in the military makes him feel like he is living a life that matters, and he hopes that it is pleasing in the sight of God.

SERGEANT HARRIS AHMAD KHAN

Sgt. Harris Ahmad Khan is 12Bravo, a military term meaning that he is a combat engineer. Combat engineers are the personnel who move at the very front of the line in ground operations. They go in first, because their job is to clear the way for the infantry in one of two ways. Those who are charged with route clearance find and dispose of IEDs. Other combat engineers, such as Khan, are tasked with breaching, the removal of any obstacle in the way of the infantry. These obstacles might include the door to a building, a berm, or a T-wall, the twelve-foot-wide blast barriers com-posed of reinforced concrete. Khan often travels in the M113 armored per-sonnel carrier, and like other combat engineers, he uses various explosives such as C4 to breach whatever barrier he finds.

From October 2015 to July 2016, Khan was part of Operation Inher-ent Resolve, the US military's effort to "eliminate the terrorist group ISIL and the threat they pose to Iraq, the region, and the wider international community."[12] President Barack Obama, who ended the Iraq War in 2011, ordered this new operation in 2014 to counter the growth of ISIL, the Is-lamic State of Iraq and the Levant, also known as ISIS and in Arabic as Da'ish (pronounced DA-ish). By 2014, Da'ish had exploited the civil war in Syria and the lack of a unified government in Iraq to become a regional political power. It controlled territory in both countries, ruling millions of people under a harsh and intolerant interpretation of Islam. Its leader, Abu Bakr al-Baghdadi, declared himself the caliph, or leader of all Muslims— his goal was to bring the entire world under the caliphate's sovereignty. Though Da'ish encouraged Muslims around the world to stage terrorist attacks on the enemies of Islam, most of its victims were Muslims living in Syria and Iraq.[13]

Khan, one of over a billion Muslims from around the world that op-poses Da'ish, was born in Chicago, Illinois. His family moved around, but his formative years as a teenager were spent in Baltimore, Maryland, where he was part of community of both African American and South Asian American Muslims.[14] His parents are ethnic Pashtuns from Pakistan. As a kid, Khan enjoyed watching military-themed cartoons and movies. By the end of his junior year, as Khan was starting to look at colleges, he decided that he wanted to serve his country. It was 2011, and the United States was still at war. He knew what he was getting into. One of his role models was Mansoor Shams, a former corporal in the marine corps who was also a youth leader at his mosque.[15] Khan felt like it was his responsibility to serve, that it was "part of being a man." His faith, he said, also made it an obligation: "As a Muslim, you have to defend and support your country."

Khan joined the navy after graduating from high school in Prince George's County, Maryland. He enjoyed it, but it wasn't what he expected. He wanted to be on the field of battle. He wanted to run and carry a weapon. Khan applied for the Operation Blue to Green program, which allows air force and navy personnel to transfer to the army.

Khan found his military home. "You sleep together, eat together, shower together," he said. These bonds mean that one solider looks out for another. It also means that there is little room for bigotry. "It doesn't matter what the color of your skin is or your religion is," he asserted. The unit can't afford threats to its unity.

Many of the soldiers who meet Khan eventually learn that he is a Muslim. For some, it is the first time they have ever talked to a Muslim. What they sometimes don't know is that he is a member of the Ahmadiyya Muslim Community. The Ahmadis are a sect of Islam distinct from Sunnis, Shias, and the Nation of Islam. They are called Ahmadi because they follow the teachings of Mirza Ghulam Ahmad (1835–1908), whom Ahmadis believe to be the Messiah, the second coming of Jesus. Sunni and Shia Muslims also believe that Jesus is the Messiah who will return to the world before the Day of Judgment, but they reject the idea that Ghulam Ahmad was a messiah. There has been an Ahmadi community in the United States since the 1920s.

Though Khan's membership in the Ahmadi community distinguishes him from most other Muslims around the world, his religious practices are largely the same as both Sunni and Shia Muslims. He regularly prays, prostrating his body in the direction of Islam's holiest shrine in Mecca, and he fasts from dawn to sunset during the Islamic holy month of Ramadan. Khan also observes the Islamic ban on eating pork, and the army accommodates this practice by making sure that he has chicken or vegetarian MREs while in combat. When there is a barbecue on base, which inevitably involves pork, someone makes sure that something else is available on the side for Khan. "My guys are always watching out for me," he said.

"I wouldn't call myself a perfect Muslim," he told me, but his faith is essential to him. Khan relies on God to get him through the tough times. "I'm a firm believer in God. If it wasn't for my faith, I wouldn't be as motivated as I am to serve. God keeps me moving when it's 130 degrees in Kuwait and I have to keep moving, when it's cold, when I'm tired."

That sentiment makes him no different than hundreds of thousands of his fellow service members who would say the same thing, no matter what their faith.

Today's Muslim American Military through the Prism of the Past

Laura Magee, Nashid Salahuddin, Jibril Smythe, and Harris Khan are extraordinary people, but their love of country and belief that their faith supports their military service are ordinary, at least in the military. Many people of faith in the military, most of them Christian, feel the same way. The loyalty of religious service members, whether they are Muslim or not, does not come from agreeing with every single decision that the Department of Defense or the president makes. It comes instead from a commitment to one's duty, a decision to abide by the oath to support and defend the US Constitution, and if they are enlisted, to obey the orders of the president and military officers. As we have seen, that oath often takes shape not in any theoretical discussion but instead in the day-to-day relationships that service members have with one another. This is where the bonds of loyalty become real.

Muslim service members, like non-Muslim service members, join the military for a variety of reasons. Many of them benefit from educational and other opportunities offered by the US military in exchange for their willingness to make the ultimate sacrifice. This is not a Muslim phenomenon; it reflects the military as a whole. Some Muslim service members, perhaps many Muslim service members, disagreed with the 2003 war in Iraq and the long-term nature of the war in Afghanistan. Yet they did their duty, hoping they could have a positive impact through their personal example. Too many had to tolerate anti-Muslim attitudes among some of their brothers- and sisters-in-arms. But they did it for the greater good of their country and their religion.

As I spoke with current service members and veterans in the course of writing this book, it became clear to me that many Muslim members of the military know some aspects of their long history but not others. Perhaps someone was familiar with Nicholas Said, but not Hadji Ali, or someone knew about service members from the Vietnam War era but did not know the stories of World War I veterans. This should not come as a surprise. Only some of these stories have been passed along. Muslims are racially and ethnically diverse, and they have a lot of different social circles and networks. Until the 1950s, Muslims did not seek recognition from the US military. It took decades for the military to recognize the first Muslim chaplain. Their history, until recently, has remained hidden.

Muslims in the US military only rose to national prominence after 9/11. Soldiers such as Kareem Khan and Humayun Khan became symbols in the cultural and political wars over what it meant to be an American. As wars raged in Muslim lands, some Americans feared Muslim service members were the enemy inside the gates, and even more, that their religion was inherently anti-American. Others hailed the blood sacrifices of Muslim military members as proof of America's special calling to defend liberty, whether at home or abroad. These were only two ways to interpret the sacrifice of Muslim service members, but they played out on the huge stage of two US presidential elections—in 2008 with Colin Powell's eulogy of Kareem Khan on "Meet the Press" and in 2016 with the speech by Humayun Khan's father.

The presidential election of 2016, especially, sent journalists and others scrambling to find information about Muslim service members. It was easy enough to interview current military members and especially living veterans, but practically no information on the long history of Muslims in the military was available. If anything, this short book should point to areas where there are more stories to be told.

Given the importance of Islam and Muslims to US politics and society, it is imperative that we Americans come to understand our current moment through the prism of the past. The past provides a space where we can let our imaginations roam as we connect to our Muslim ancestors. We can compare their stories to those of other religious, racial, and ethnic minorities in the US military. We can see ourselves reflected in the lives of all these ancestors, not just one race or class or religion. There is a reason why so many Americans participate in military reenactments. Military life—its violence and discipline and honor—remains central to who we are as a people.

It is well past time to include the stories, the good and the bad, of Muslim military members in that larger collective narrative. When we talk about Muslims in the military, we should remember Bilali Mahomet on Sapelo Island armed with a musket, ready to repel the British. We should think about what Hadji Ali's life as a camel driver must have been like, and we should marvel at the amazing intellect of Sgt. Nicholas Said. We should imagine Pvt. Omer Otmen at the Battle of Meuse Argonne in World War I and John Omar taking shrapnel in his foot as he pried open his B-24's bomb doors. If we remember enough of their stories and tell them in a realistic way, we can begin to see Muslims in the military as fully human rather than as mere symbols. We can dream of a time when Muslims mothers and fathers can oppose the wars in which their sons and daughters are fighting, without considering them disloyal. We can even look with respect at those Muslim Americans such as Muhammad Ali who have refused to serve in the military. If we are good enough listeners, we can empathize with all of these people, whether we agree with them or not.

As the US military remains engaged with both enemies and allies that happen to be Muslim, contemplating the long history of Muslims in the US military is an opportunity to avoid the easy and dangerous thinking that sees Muslims and their religion as the enemy of America. But it goes beyond that. It is also an opportunity to take stock of US foreign policy around the world and think about the implications of those policies through the sometimes troubling, sometimes heroic, sometimes mundane lives of service members such as Fatima Ahmed, Shareda Hosein, James Yee, Abraham Al-Thaibani, Nashid Salahuddin, and Laura Magee. Even without knowing them completely, we can still ponder whether we as a people want to put them and all other members of the military in harm's way. At the very least, when the decision to go to war is made, we should remember that thousands of Muslim American service members will follow their orders and will fight for the United States, just as they have done for more than two centuries.

Notes

1. Mohamed Younis, "Perceptions of Muslims in the United States: A Review," Gallup, December 11, 2015, http://www.gallup.com/opinion/gallup/187664/perceptions-muslims-united-states-review.aspx.

2. Shareda Hosein, "Military: Women's Participation, United States," in *Encyclopedia of Women and Islamic Cultures*, vol. 2, ed. Suad Joseph (2005), http://sjoseph.ucdavis.edu/ewic-public-outreach-resources/ewic-outreach-resources/military-womens-participation-united-states.

3. Mariam Khan and Luis Martinez, "More than 5,000 Muslims Serving in US Military, Pentagon Says," ABC News, Dec. 8, 2015, http://abcnews.go.com/US/5000-muslims-serving-us-military-pentagon/story?id=35654904.

4. Hosein, "Military: Women's Participation, United States."

5. The following account is based on Laura Magee, "Chaplain's Corner," *High Roller News* 26, no. 8 (August 2016): 15, 17, http://www.152aw.ang.af.mil/shared/media/document/AFD-160803-002.pdf.

6. The story of the conversion is told in Laura Magee, "As-Salaamu Alaykum," *For the Love of the Deen* (blog), January 23, 2016, http://fortheloveofdeen.blogspot.com/2016/01/as-salaamu-alaykum.html.

7. Reactions to Magee's conversion are detailed in Laura Magee, "What? You're Muslim?!?" *For the Love of the Deen* (blog), August 20, 2016, http://fortheloveofdeen.blogspot.com/2016_08_01_archive.html.

8. Laura Magee, "Chaplain's Corner," *High Roller News* 25, no. 2 (February 2015): 10, http://www.152aw.ang.af.mil/shared/media/document/AFD-150206-055.pdf.

9. Laura Magee, "Chaplain's Corner," *High Roller News* 26, no. 3 (March 2016): 15, http://www.152aw.ang.af.mil/shared/media/document/AFD-160302-077.pdf.

10. Sources for my account of Col. Nashid Salahuddin include a phone interview that I conducted on August 12, 2016, and Karen Rester, "Muslim American Nashid Salahuddin Serves God and Country," *Muslim Journal*, Nov. 15, 2011, http://muslimjournal.net/muslim-american-nashid-salahuddin-serves-god-and-country-by-karen-rester/.

11. Jibril Smythe is a pseudonym, inspired by one of James Bond's pseudonyms, St. John Smythe in *A View to a Kill*. I interviewed Smythe via telephone on August 16, 2016.

12. US Department of Defense, Operation Inherent Resolve, http://www.inherentresolve.mil.

13. Ibid.

14. My account of Harris Khan's service is based on a phone interview conducted on August 30, 2016, and subsequent email correspondence on August 31, 2016.

15. For more on Mansoor Shams, see his website, Muslim Marine, http://www.muslimmarine.org/.

INDEX

Page numbers in italics indicate illustrations.

EDWARD E. CURTIS IV is the author
of several books, including *Muslims
in America: A Short History.*

CPSIA information can be obtained
at www.ICGtesting.com
Printed in the USA
BVOW06s0937161216

471016BV00020B/242/P